charm school

18 QUILTS FROM 5″ SQUARES

a beginner's guide

VANESSA GOERTZEN OF LELLA BOUTIQUE

stashBOOKS.
an imprint of C&T Publishing

Text copyright © 2017 by Vanessa Goertzen

Photography and artwork copyright © 2017 by C&T Publishing, Inc.

Publisher: Amy Marson

Creative Director: Gailen Runge

Editors: Lynn Koolish and Monica Gyulai

Technical Editors: Del Walker and Debbie Rodgers

Cover/Book Designer: April Mostek

Production Coordinators: Zinnia Heinzmann and Tim Manibusan

Production Editors: Nicole Rolandelli and Jennifer Warren

Illustrator: Freesia Pearson Blizard

Photo Assistants: Carly Jean Marin and Mai Yong Vang

Style photography by Lucy Glover and instructional photography by Diane Pedersen, unless otherwise noted

Published by Stash Books, an imprint of C&T Publishing, Inc., P.O. Box 1456, Lafayette, CA 94549

Library of Congress Cataloging-in-Publication Data

Names: Goertzen, Vanessa, 1984- author.

Title: Charm school--18 quilts from 5″ squares : a beginner's guide / Vanessa Goertzen.

Description: Lafayette, CA : C&T Publishing, Inc., [2017]

Identifiers: LCCN 2016025934 | ISBN 9781617452710 (soft cover)

Subjects: LCSH: Patchwork quilts. | Patchwork--Patterns. | Quilting.

Classification: LCC TT835 .G332464 2017 | DDC 746.46--dc23

LC record available at https://lccn.loc.gov/2016025934

Printed in the USA

10 9 8

dedication

To Olive and Lorenzo, my favorite snugglers, who dance the hokey pokey with me every night before bed. You are the best that a mama could wish for.

To my amazing mother, for sharing her time and talents with me since I was young. Thank you for teaching me how to play with fabric, use a sewing machine, and run wild with my ideas. You are one of my greatest treasures.

To my family and friends, for always cheering me on in my crazy endeavors. This is for you.

Photo by Peekaboophotos

acknowledgments

Thank you to Abby and Natalia, my wonderful friends and quilters. You have transformed my quilt designs into veritable works of art.

I fell in love with Moda Fabrics long before I worked for them. Thank you to all the wonderful people there—especially Mark, Lissa, Cheryl, and Jamie. It is a dream come true to work with you.

A special thanks to Riley Blake Designs, Marcus Fabrics, Cotton + Steel, and Art Gallery Fabrics for allowing me to use your beautiful fabric collections.

Thanks to Alex at Aurifil for the superb thread; to Prym and OLFA, for your amazing tools, which make the cutting process so much easier; and to Fairfield, for your wonderful Nature-Fil batting—the unseen but vital part of making a quilt come to life.

To my dear friend, Susan, for being my second pair of eyes and providing invaluable input.

Finally, thank you, C&T Publishing—especially Amy, April, Carly, Debbie, Del, Diane, Freesia, Gailen, Jennifer, Lucy, Lynn, Mai, Monica, Nicole, Roxane, Tim, and Zinnia—for your hard work and support in making this book come to life.

contents

keeping it square   14

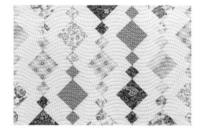
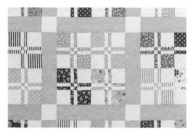

rectangle blocks   30

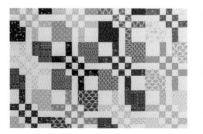
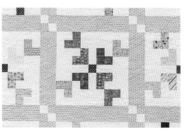

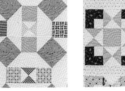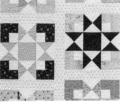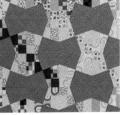
Finishing the Quilt 124

Preparing the backing fabric • Batting • Basting • Quilting • Binding

About the Author 127

Charm School—18 Quilts from 5" Squares

INTRODUCTION

When I was pregnant with my first child and found out I was having a girl, I went straight to the quilt shop next door to start looking for fabric. I found a few perfect fat quarters and then happened to notice the sweet little precut bundles of 5″ × 5″ squares called charm packs. I had never seen them before and was so enchanted by them that I grabbed a couple, just to see what I could make.

I found that playing with these 5″ × 5″ squares was such fun—and that there were endless possibilities for what I could do with them. I used them like building blocks and discovered a whole new world of creativity.

I hope you'll join me at my Charm School. In my mother's time, charm school was a place young ladies attended in heels and hose—to learn perfect table manners and ways to become socially brilliant. At my Charm School, you will learn to work with precut charm squares, and, if you wish, to use fat quarters or scraps to make your own 5″ × 5″ squares. The project directions include all the information you need. The best part is that you don't need heels and hose—while attending my Charm School, you are cordially invited to work in your pajamas or your jeans!

While basic information is included for beginning quiltmakers, I've presented quilts for all levels of experience. Start with the 5″ × 5″ squares, just the way they are, and gradually learn how to make simple alterations. Half-Square Triangles will make your designs more interesting and fun. Read the lessons and hints to help you put the quilts together quickly. Each of the chapters builds on techniques introduced in previous chapters. As you progress in the book, you'll practice techniques you have already learned and also learn new ones.

Basic instructions on finishing (layering, basting, quilting, and binding) are included to help you complete the process. Look through the entire book before you start so that you have a visual picture of the possibilities and techniques. By the time you finish making several of the quilts in this book, you'll be ready to graduate from Charm School.

SELECTING THE FABRIC

The thing I love most about using 5″ × 5″ squares is that there are many ways to cut them from fabric. Even though precut charm squares were my inspiration for the projects in this book, it is very easy to substitute fat quarters or even scraps. Don't hesitate to make your own charm packs. Choose what you'd like and get started.

charm packs

A charm pack is a little bundle of precut 5″ × 5″ squares. The wonderful things about charm packs are the convenience and the fabric selection. Within each charm pack, you'll find an assortment of coordinating prints curated by a professional designer. And, of course, the cutting has already been done, so you can begin to use those 5″ × 5″ squares right away.

Charm packs are produced by a number of manufacturers—although the manufacturers may market them under a different name. In this book I use the Moda Fabrics brand of charm packs as the standard, since Moda charm packs always contain 42 precut 5″ × 5″ squares per bundle. This is important to remember if you use a different manufacturer's version. Check how many squares are in your precut bundle and adjust the number you purchase accordingly.

fat quarters

I always have a great time creating my own special mix of fabrics when choosing fat quarters. Sometimes I pick my favorites within one fabric collection, or I might create a totally unique assortment from several groups. When substituting fat quarters for charm packs, you won't have as wide a variety of prints. This works well when you're going for a less scrappy look.

A fat quarter measures 18″ × 22″. It is a quarter-yard of fabric, just as is a piece measuring 9″ × 44″. But a chunk is sometimes more useful to quilters than a strip. This is especially true when it comes to cutting 5″ × 5″ squares. For example, a fat quarter can be cut into twelve squares 5″ × 5″, whereas a skinny quarter-yard will yield only eight squares.

Visit your local quilt shop. Most shops will cut fat quarters from the bolt if you don't find what you need in their precut selection.

scraps

Most quilters accumulate a lot of scraps over the years, but they don't always have a lot of room for them. I like to keep a pile of 5″ × 5″ square leftovers so I can assemble my own charm packs. Look through your stash and see what you can come up with!

Cutting Charm Squares from Precuts and Yardage

- You can cut 10″ × 10″ precut squares (also called layer cakes, stackers, or stack packs) into 4 charm squares.

- You can cut 5″ × WOF precut strips (also called charm rolls, dessert rolls, or fat rolls) into 8 charm squares.

CHARM SQUARE CUTTING FROM YARDAGE

Yardage	Number of Charm Squares
Skinny quarter-yard (9″ × 40″–42″)	8
Fat quarter-yard (18″ × 22″)	12
½ yard (18″ × 40″–42″)	24
¾ yard (27″ × 40″–42″)	40
1 yard (36″ × 40″–42″)	56

TOOLS AND SUPPLIES

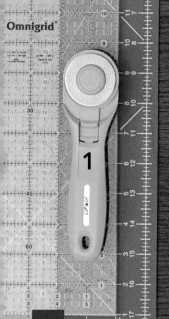

As a busy mother of young children, I am glad I live during a time when there are so many wonderful tools available to make quilting a quick and convenient process. Because quilting relies heavily on precision cutting and piecing, I find the following tools essential to success.

cutting

1. Rotary cutter

2. Self-healing cutting mat (24″ × 36″)

3. Acrylic rulers, 6″ × 24″ and 6″ × 12″; 4½″ Bloc Loc ruler

piecing

4. Sewing machine

5. Steam iron

6. ¼″ quilter's foot

7. Quality thread

8. Marking pencils or heat-removable marking pens

9. Fabric scissors (8″)

10. Small scissors for clipping threads

11. Glass-head pins

12. Seam ripper

basting, quilting, and binding

13. Batting

14. Safety pins

15. Rubber fingertips (also known as finger cots) or quilting gloves for free-motion quilting

16. Darning foot for free-motion quilting

17. Walking foot

18. Needles for hand sewing

note

Vanessa's Favorites

Not all tools and supplies are created equal, and I always try to use the best. Below are some of the specific brands I trust and love.

✗ OLFA Splash 45 mm rotary cutter

✗ Omnigrid Mat (24″ × 36″) with grid

✗ Omnigrid acrylic rulers (6″ × 12″ and 6″ × 24″)

✗ BERNINA 550 QE (Quilter's Edition) sewing machine

✗ Aurifil 50wt thread

✗ Gingher 8″ shears

✗ Fairfield Nature-Fil bamboo/cotton-blend batting

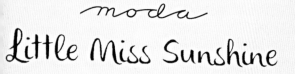

moda

Little Miss Sunshine

by Vanessa Goertzen of Lella Boutique for *moda*

moda

*CORAL*Queen of the Sea

STACY IEST HSU for *moda*

BEFORE YOU BEGIN

Before you start cutting and sewing, here are a few basic terms and techniques used in the book.

width of fabric (WOF)

Quilting cottons usually measure 42″–44″ wide off the bolt, depending on the manufacturer. All fabric calculations in this book assume a 40″ fabric width, just to ensure that you will have enough. Sometimes *width of fabric* is abbreviated as *WOF*.

right sides together (RST)

Seams are generally sewn with "right sides together," or with the printed sides of the fabric pieces facing each other. If not instructed otherwise, sew all seams with right sides together. *Right sides together* can be abbreviated as *RST*.

pressing

Pressing is an important step in the piecing process. I like to use a steam iron—a shot of steam can really help seams stay flat. There are a couple of ways to press seams:

1. Open **Fig. A**

2. To one side, usually toward the darker fabric **Fig. B**

Both methods have their place, so you will find both used throughout this book. Pay close attention to the pressing directions specified within each project's instructions.

a

mastering the ¼″ seam

Piecing a quilt block is a precise art and depends on sewing accurate ¼″ seams. Be sure to test and measure the exactness of your ¼″ seam. A quilter's foot is a marvelous tool, and there are other products aiming to help quilters achieve ¼″ perfection. Even with a quilter's foot, I have found that I get the best results using a scant ¼″ seam allowance, to take into account the tiny bulk added by the thread and the pressing method.

b

keeping it square

So many design possibilities exist for using just the little 5″ × 5″ square. In this section the focus is on keeping it simple. Some of the projects use the 5″ × 5″ square as is, but you'll also see how simple subcutting, fabric choice, and block setting can completely elevate the 5″ × 5″ square into something extraordinary, as in Chandelier (page 20) and Lickety-Split (page 25).

USING CHARM SQUARES

Keep the 5″ × 5″ square as is, sewing together the whole squares.

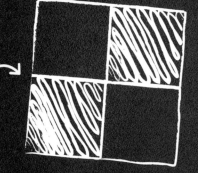

Subcut the 5″ × 5″ square into 4 squares 2½″ × 2½″. Combine with a 5″ × 5″ square to get new block designs.

MODERN BASIC

finished block: 13½˝ × 13½˝ • *finished quilt:* 81˝ × 81˝

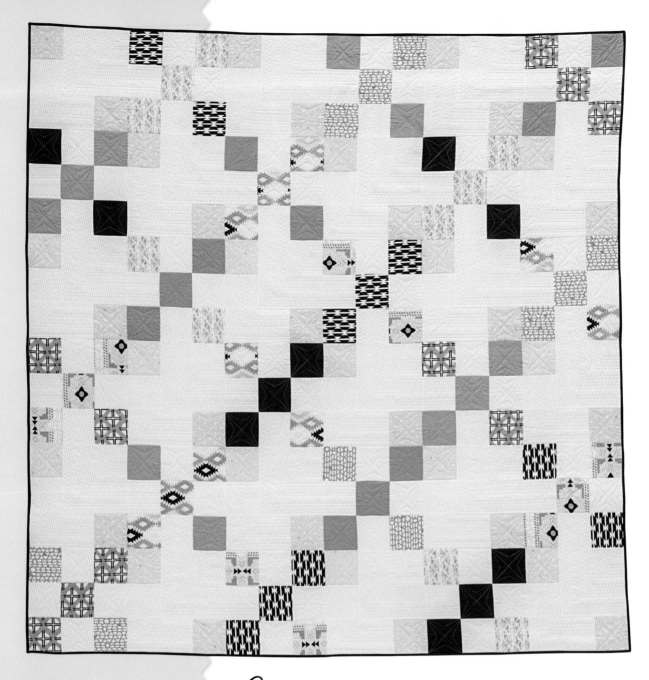

pieced by
Vanessa Goertzen

quilted by
Natalia Bonner

*Fabric: Arizona
by April Rhodes
for Art Gallery Fabrics*

One of the things I love about simple quilts is the opportunity to let beautiful fabric do all the talking. Of course, it doesn't get any simpler than a basic block quilt—and this one uses graphic prints and solids from April Rhodes's Arizona collection to make a bold statement. Add to that some stunning custom quilting and you have a masterpiece.

materials

3 charm packs *or* 9 fat quarters *or* scraps

⅞ yard of mint fabric

4 yards of white fabric

7½ yards of backing fabric

¾ yard of binding fabric

89″ × 89″ batting

cutting

For the blocks

3 charm packs

- No subcutting is needed. Organize the charm squares by print (there will be multiples of 3). Sort them into 18 sets of 3 for Group A. Sort the remaining charm squares into 18 sets of 2 for Group B.

9 fat quarters

From each fat quarter:

- Cut 3 strips 5″ × 22″; subcut the strips into 10 squares 5″ × 5″.

Sort the 10 squares into 2 sets of 3 (Group A) and 2 sets of 2 (Group B) for 18 sets total.

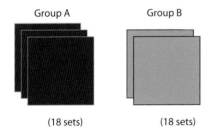

Group A (18 sets)   Group B (18 sets)

Scraps

- Cut or gather 18 sets of 3 squares 5″ × 5″ of the same (or a similar) print for Group A. Cut or gather 18 sets of 2 squares 5″ × 5″ of the same (or a similar) print for Group B.

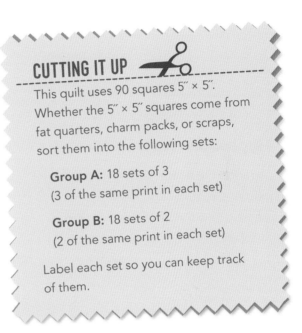

CUTTING IT UP

This quilt uses 90 squares 5″ × 5″. Whether the 5″ × 5″ squares come from fat quarters, charm packs, or scraps, sort them into the following sets:

Group A: 18 sets of 3
(3 of the same print in each set)

Group B: 18 sets of 2
(2 of the same print in each set)

Label each set so you can keep track of them.

Mint fabric

- Cut 5 strips 5″ × WOF. Subcut into 5″ × 5″ squares, 8 per strip, until you have 36.

White fabric

- Cut 5 strips 9½″ × WOF. Subcut into 9½″ × 9½″ squares, 4 per strip, until you have 18.

- Cut 5 strips 5″ × WOF. Subcut into 5″ × 9½″ rectangles, 4 per strip, until you have 18.

- Cut 12 strips 5″ × WOF. Subcut into 5″ × 5″ squares, 8 per strip, until you have 90.

Binding fabric

- Cut 9 strips 2½″ × WOF.

construction ✑

Seam allowances are ¼˝ unless otherwise noted. Arrows indicate pressing direction. Sew fabrics with right sides together.

MAKE THE BLOCKS

Nine-Patches

1. To make 1 block, gather the following:

  1 set of 3 from Group A

  1 set of 2 from Group B

  4 white squares 5˝ × 5˝

2. Arrange the 5˝ × 5˝ squares from Group A, Group B, and the white fabric as shown. Sew the blocks into rows and press. Sew the rows together and press. Make 18. **Fig. A**

Accent Blocks

1. To make 1 block, gather the following:

  2 mint squares 5˝ × 5˝

  1 white square 5˝ × 5˝

  1 white rectangle 5˝ × 9½˝

  1 white square 9½˝ × 9½˝

2. Sew 1 mint square 5˝ × 5˝ to 1 white square 5˝ × 5˝. **Fig. B**

3. Attach the unit from Step 2 to the right side of the white 9½˝ × 9½˝ square. **Fig. C**

4. Sew the remaining mint square 5˝ × 5˝ to the white rectangle 5˝ × 9½˝ and add it to the top of the pieced unit from Step 3. Make 18. **Fig. D**

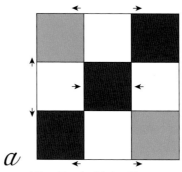

a

Nine-Patch. Make 18.

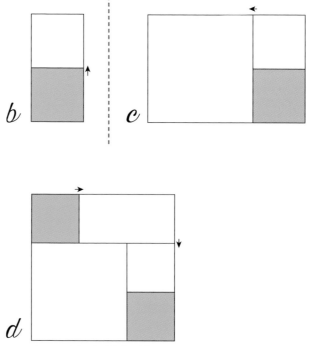

b *c*

d

Accent block. Make 18.

PUT IT TOGETHER

1. Arrange the Nine-Patches and Accent blocks into 6 rows of 6 blocks, as shown.

2. Sew the blocks into rows and press.

3. Sew together the rows and press.

FINISH

Baste, quilt, and bind using your preferred method, or refer to Finishing the Quilt (page 124).

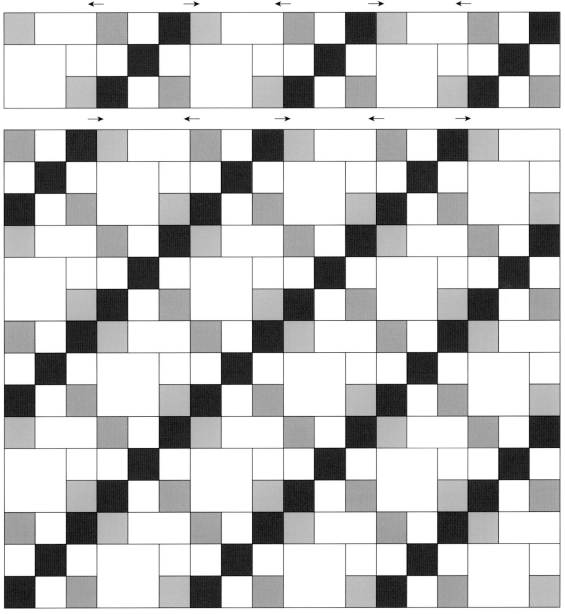

Quilt assembly

CHANDELIER

finished block : 8½″ × 8½″ • *finished quilt* : 60″ × 60″

materials

2 charm packs *or* 7 fat quarters *or* scraps

3 yards of cream background fabric

4 yards of backing fabric

⅝ yard of binding fabric

68″ × 68″ batting

cutting

For the blocks

2 charm packs

- Organize the charm squares into 41 matching pairs. From each pair, reserve 1 square 5″ × 5″ and subcut 2 squares 2½″ × 2½″ from the other.

7 fat quarters

From each fat quarter:

- Cut 2 strips 5″ × 22″ and subcut into 6 squares 5″ × 5″. Cut 2 strips 2½″ × 22″ and subcut into 12 squares 2½″ × 2½″. Organize the squares by print.

Scraps

- Gather or cut 41 sets, with each set containing 1 square 5″ × 5″ and 2 squares 2½″ × 2½″ of the same (or a similar) print.

Cream background fabric

- Cut 2 strips 13⅜″ × WOF. Subcut each strip into 2 squares 13⅜″ × 13⅜″ and 1 square 6⅞″ × 6⅞″. Subcut each 13⅜″ × 13⅜″ square into 4 triangles by cutting along both diagonal lines to yield 16 side triangles total.

Subcut each 6⅞″ × 6⅞″ square into 2 triangles by cutting along one diagonal line to yield 4 corner triangles total.

- Cut 17 strips 2½″ × WOF. Subcut into 2½″ × 7″ rectangles, 5 per strip, until you have 82.
- Cut 11 strips 2½″ × WOF. Subcut into 2½″ × 5″ rectangles, 8 per strip, until you have 82.

Binding fabric

- Cut 7 strips 2½″ × WOF.

CUTTING IT UP ✂

This quilt uses 41 sets. Each set is 1 square 5″ × 5″ and 2 squares 2½″ × 2½″ per print.

pieced by
Vanessa Goertzen

quilted by
Abby Latimer

*Fabric: Chatsworth
by Emily Taylor
for Riley Blake Designs*

*W*hile I sew, I often watch—or listen—to a movie. One of my favorite feel-good movies, Pollyanna, *is one I used to watch at my grandma's house in Colorado. I love the scene when Pollyanna visits a recluse and notices rainbows on his walls. He explains to her that the crystals on his lamp act as prisms, refracting the ordinary sunlight into little rainbows that dance throughout the room. The look of this quilt magically changes, too, just by turning the blocks on point. This orientation lets the light dance through the shapes in a completely different manner, giving it a modern twist.*

construction

Seam allowances are ¼″ unless otherwise noted. Arrows indicate pressing direction. Sew fabrics with right sides together.

MAKE THE BLOCKS

Seven-Patches

1. To make 1 block, gather the following:

    1 square 5″ × 5″ of Print 1

    2 squares 2½″ × 2½″ of Print 1

    2 cream rectangles 2½″ × 5″

    2 cream rectangles 2½″ × 7″

2. Sew 2 cream rectangles 2½″ × 5″ to the sides of 1 square 5″ × 5″ of Print 1. **Fig. A**

3. Sew 1 cream rectangle 2½″ × 7″ to 1 square 2½″ × 2½″ of Print 1. Make 2. **Fig. B**

4. Arrange the units from Steps 2 and 3 into rows, as shown. Sew together the rows and press. **Fig. C**

5. Repeat Steps 1–4, using each matching print pair to make 41 blocks.

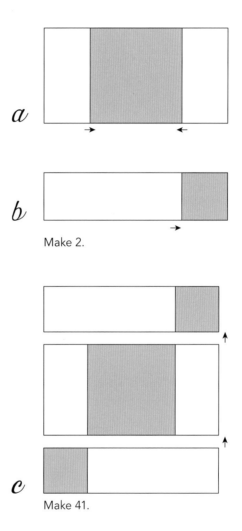

a

b

Make 2.

c

Make 41.

PUT IT TOGETHER

1. Arrange the Seven-Patches, side triangles, and corner triangles on point, as shown. Sew the blocks into rows and press.

2. Sew together the rows and press.

FINISH

Baste, quilt, and bind using your preferred method, or refer to Finishing the Quilt (page 124).

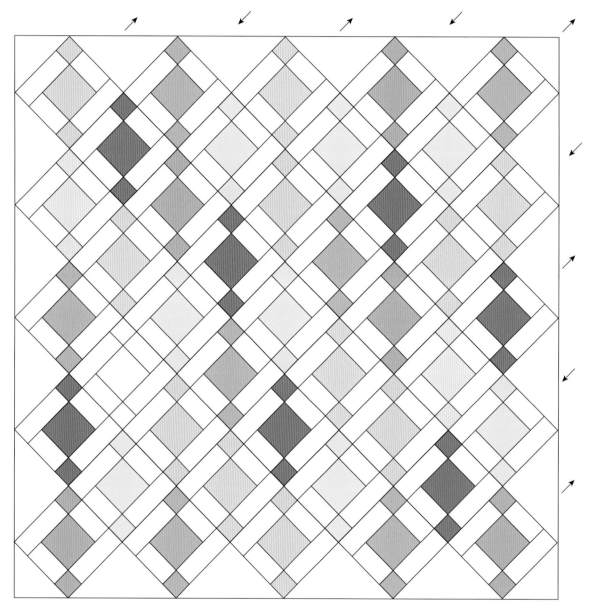

Quilt assembly

LICKETY-SPLIT

finished block: 8″ × 8″ • *finished quilt*: 62½″ × 62½″

pieced by
Vanessa Goertzen

quilted by
Abby Latimer

*Fabric: Prairie
by Corey Yoder
for Moda Fabrics*

My mother once told me that when she got mad, she could clean the house in about 30 minutes. We laugh about that, but she always figured that a dirty house was a barrier to what she really wanted to spend her time doing, and that's why she cleaned it fast. After the house was picked up, she spent the rest of the day at her sewing machine. This little quilt reminds me of the old linoleum pattern we had to scrub before we could quilt and all the fun we used to have as we rushed to get it clean.

materials

2 charm packs *or* 6 fat quarters *or* scraps

1⅝ yards of white fabric

1½ yards of yellow sashing fabric

4 yards of backing fabric

¾ yard of binding fabric

71″ × 71″ batting

cutting

For the blocks

2 charm packs

- No subcutting is needed. Organize the charm squares by print into 36 sets of 2. (There will be leftovers.)

6 fat quarters

From each fat quarter:

- Cut 3 strips 5″ × WOF; subcut into 12 squares 5″ × 5″. Organize the squares by print into 36 sets of 2.

Scraps

- Gather or cut 36 sets of 2 squares 5″ × 5″ of the same (or a similar) print.

White fabric

- Cut 9 strips 5″ × WOF. Subcut into 5″ × 5″ squares, 8 per strip, until you have 72.

- Cut 2 strips 4″ × WOF. Subcut into 4″ × 4″ squares, 10 per strip, until you have 16.

Yellow sashing fabric

- Cut 12 strips 4″ × WOF. Subcut into 4″ × 16½″ rectangles, 2 per strip, until you have 24.

Binding fabric

- Cut 7 strips 2½″ × WOF.

CUTTING IT UP ✂

This quilt uses 72 squares 5″ × 5″. Whether the 5″ × 5″ squares come from charm packs, fat quarters, or scraps, sort the squares into 36 sets of 2 (2 of the same print in each set).

construction

Seam allowances are ¼″ unless otherwise noted. Arrows indicate pressing direction. Sew fabrics with right sides together.

MAKE THE BLOCKS

Disappearing Four-to-Nine Patches

1. To make 1 block, gather the following:

    2 print squares 5″ × 5″

    2 white squares 5″ × 5″

2. Arrange the squares from Step 1 as shown. Sew the squares into rows and press. **Fig. A**

3. Sew the rows together and press open the seam. Each four-patch should measure 9½″ × 9½″. **Fig. B**

4. Place the four-patch onto your cutting mat so the seams line up with the cutting lines. Carefully cut apart the four-patch into 9 pieces by cutting 1″ away from all seams. **Fig. C**

5. Rearrange the center rectangular units of each side by rotating them 180°. Sew the units back into rows and press open the seams.

6. Sew together the rows and press open the seams. Make 36 Four-to-Nine Patches. **Fig. D**

7. Sew 4 units from Step 6 together as shown. Make 9. **Fig. E**

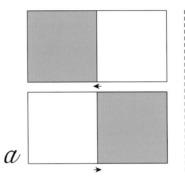

a

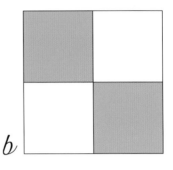

b

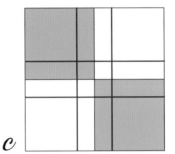

c

Cut 1″ from seams, as shown in red.

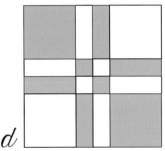

d

Four-to-Nine Patch assembly. Make 36.

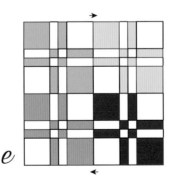

e

Block assembly. Make 9.

PUT IT TOGETHER

1. Arrange the 9 blocks from Step 7, the white squares 4″ × 4″, and the yellow sashing strips 4″ × 16½″, as shown. Sew the units into rows and press toward the yellow sashing.

2. Sew the rows together and press toward the yellow sashing.

FINISH

Baste, quilt, and bind using your preferred method, or refer to Finishing the Quilt (page 124).

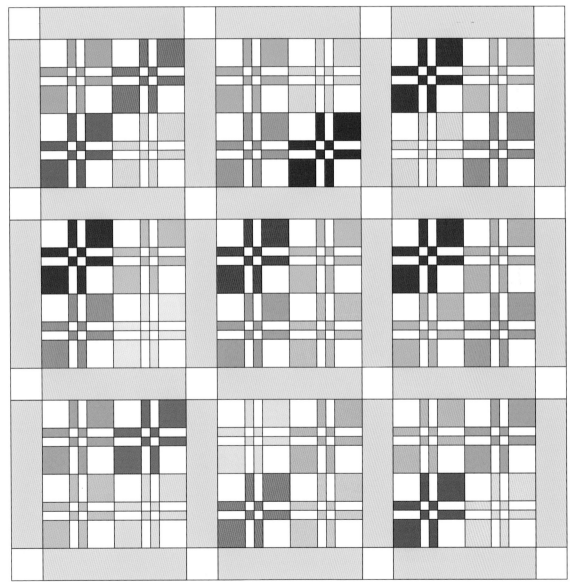

Quilt assembly

rectangle blocks

Now that you are comfortable using the basic squares, try slicing them into rectangles—and discover new design possibilities. When you line up rectangles in rows and stitch them together, they are transformed into a coin quilt. Or skip the tradition of rows and create an intersecting group of lines, as in Railroad Crossing (page 31). Then explore ways to use rectangles to create more complex shapes. One of my favorite quilts in this section is Snowfall (page 41)—it's a great example of the extraordinary potential of just rectangles and squares!

USING CHARM SQUARES

Subcut the 5″ × 5″ square into 2 rectangles 2½″ × 5″.
Sew the rectangles into rows to make a coin quilt.

Combine 5″ × 5″ squares, 2½″ × 2½″ squares, and 2½″ × 5″ rectangles to make new blocks.

RAILROAD CROSSING

finished block: 12½˝ × 12½˝ • *finished quilt:* 71½˝ × 84˝

pieced and quilted by
Vanessa Goertzen

*Fabric: Feed Company
by Sweetwater
for Moda Fabrics*

When my mom was a young girl, she lived next to a railroad track way out in the country. She and her siblings often went out to see the train when it thundered past, belching smoke and offering a wonderful variety of colored boxcars. In the summertime when I was a girl, I built my own memories of watching the train pass by when I went out to the tracks. This quilt conjures up memories of the foundation of railroad ties and uses 5″ × 5″ squares both as a center block at the intersections and as a subcut to make the railroad line between the squares.

materials

4 charm packs *or* 13 fat quarters *or* scraps

2 yards of white fabric

1¼ yards of border fabric

5¼ yards of backing fabric

¾ yard of binding fabric

80″ × 92″ batting

cutting

For the blocks

4 charm packs

- Select 120 squares (60 matching pairs) and subcut in half to yield 240 rectangles 2½″ × 5″. (Keep them sorted by print in sets of 4.) From the remaining charm squares, select 30 squares and set them aside for the block centers.

13 fat quarters

From each fat quarter:

- Cut 12 squares 5″ × 5″ until you have 150 total. Select 120 squares (60 matching pairs) and subcut each in half to yield 240 rectangles 2½″ × 5″. (Keep them sorted by print in sets of 4.) From the remaining charm squares, select 30 squares and set them aside for the block centers.

Scraps

- Gather or cut 30 squares 5″ × 5″ for the block centers and 120 squares 5″ × 5″ (60 matching pairs) to subcut into 240 rectangles 2½″ × 5″. (Keep them sorted by print in sets of 4.)

CUTTING IT UP

This quilt uses 150 squares 5″ × 5″. Whether the 5″ × 5″ squares come from charm packs, fat quarters, or scraps, you will need to select 120 squares (60 matching pairs) and subcut each in half to yield 240 rectangles 2½″ × 5″. (Keep them sorted by print in sets of 4.) From the remaining charm squares, select 30 squares and set them aside for the block centers.

White fabric

- Cut 15 strips 4½″ × WOF. Subcut into 4½″ × 4½″ squares, 8 per strip, until you have 120.

Border fabric

- Cut 8 strips 5″ × WOF. Piece together in pairs along short sides to make 4 border strips.

Binding fabric

- Cut 8 strips 2½″ × WOF.

construction

Seam allowances are ¼″ unless otherwise noted. Arrows indicate pressing direction. Sew fabrics with right sides together.

MAKE THE BLOCKS

Railroad Nine-Patches

1. To make 1 block, gather the following:

  1 square 5″ × 5″ for block center

  1 set of 4 rectangles 2½″ × 5″ of Print 1

  1 set of 4 rectangles 2½″ × 5″ of Print 2

  4 white squares 4½″ × 4½″

2. Arrange all units as shown. Sew together the 2½″ × 5″ rectangles in pairs, press toward the darker print, and place back into the block arrangement. Sew the blocks into rows and press. Sew the rows together and press toward the center row. Make 30.

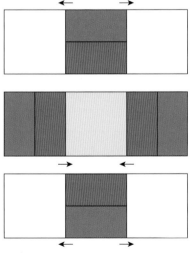

Make 30.

PUT IT TOGETHER

1. Arrange the Railroad Nine-Patch blocks into 6 rows of 5 blocks as shown. Sew the blocks into rows and press.

2. Sew together the rows and press.

BORDER

1. Measure the length of the quilt in several places to determine the average. Trim 2 border strips to match your measurement and sew to the right and left sides of the quilt. Press.

2. Repeat this process for the top and bottom borders.

FINISH

Baste, quilt, and bind using your preferred method, or refer to Finishing the Quilt (page 124).

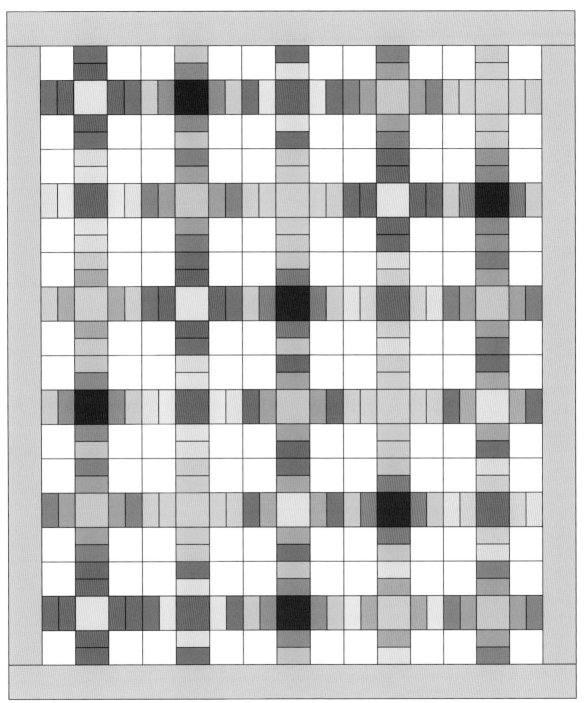

Quilt assembly

CAT'S CRADLE

finished block: 15″ × 15″ • *finished quilt:* 69″ × 84″

materials

4 charm packs *or* 12 fat quarters *or* scraps

3¼ yards of white fabric

5¼ yards of backing fabric

¾ yard of binding fabric

77″ × 92″ batting

cutting

For the blocks

4 charm packs

- Combine and organize the charm pack squares by print (there will be multiples of 4). Sort them into sets and subcut as directed.

  Group A: 20 sets of 4 squares 5″ × 5″. Keep 2 squares 5″ × 5″. Subcut 2 squares into 4 rectangles 2½″ × 5″.

  Group B: 20 sets of 3 squares 5″ × 5″. Subcut 2 squares into 4 rectangles 2½″ × 5″; subcut the 1 remaining square into 4 squares 2½″ × 2½″.

12 fat quarters

- Group A: From each of 7 fat quarters, cut 6 squares 5″ × 5″ and 12 rectangles 2½″ × 5″.

- Group B: From each of 5 fat quarters, cut 16 rectangles 2½″ × 5″ and 16 squares 2½″ × 2½″.

Scraps

- Group A: Gather or cut 20 sets, with each set containing 2 squares 5″ × 5″ and 4 rectangles 2½″ × 5″ of the same (or a similar) print.

- Group B: Gather or cut 20 sets, with each set containing 4 rectangles 2½″ × 5″ and 4 squares 2½″ × 2½″ of the same (or a similar) print.

CUTTING IT UP

This quilt uses 140 squares 5″ × 5″. Whether the 5″ × 5″ squares come from charm packs, fat quarters, or scraps, sort them into the following sets:

Group A: 20 sets of 4 (4 of the same print in each set). Within each set, subcut 2 of the 5″ × 5″ squares into 4 rectangles 2½″ × 5″. Keep the 2 remaining squares 5″ × 5″.

Group B: 20 sets of 3 (3 of the same print in each set). Within each set, subcut 2 of the 5″ × 5″ squares into 4 rectangles 2½″ × 5″. Subcut the remaining 5″ × 5″ squares into 4 squares 2½″ × 2½″.

Label each set so you can keep track of them.

White fabric

- Cut 8 strips 5″ × WOF. Piece together in pairs along the short sides to make 4 border strips.

- Cut 5 strips 5″ × WOF. Subcut into 5″ × 5″ squares, 8 per strip, until you have 40.

- Cut 10 strips 2½″ × WOF. Subcut into 2½″ × 5″ rectangles, 8 per strip, until you have 80.

- Cut 7 strips 2½″ × WOF. Subcut into 2½″ × 2½″ squares, 16 per strip, until you have 100.

Binding fabric

- Cut 9 strips 2½″ × WOF.

pieced by
Vanessa Goertzen

quilted by
Abby Latimer

Fabric: Valley
by Sherri & Chelsi
for Moda Fabrics

*K*eeping little fingers busy is often a mom's best strategy for creating peace and happiness in the house. We all know boredom fosters naughtiness— and that can be true for adults, too. My mother used to give us embroidery floss to weave bracelets for our best friends. We also had strings that we would use to play cat's cradle. When you make this quilt, think of those little childhood games as you look at the shapes created by the placement of the colors.

construction

Seam allowances are ¼″ unless otherwise noted. Press open the seams. Sew fabrics with right sides together.

MAKE THE BLOCKS

Cat's Cradle Block

1. To make 1 block, gather the following:

1 set of Group A (2 squares 5″ × 5″ and 4 rectangles 2½″ × 5″ of Print 1)

1 set of Group B (4 rectangles 2½″ × 5″ and 4 squares 2½″ × 2½″ of Print 2)

2 white squares 5″ × 5″

4 white rectangles 2½″ × 5″

5 white squares 2½″ × 2½″

2. Arrange 4 squares 2½″ × 2½″ of Print 2 with 5 white squares 2½″ × 2½″ to form a Nine-Patch, as shown. Sew the squares into rows and press. **Fig. A**

3. Sew together the rows and press.

4. Arrange 1 rectangle 2½″ × 5″ of Print 1, 1 white rectangle 2½″ × 5″, and 1 rectangle 2½″ × 5″ of Print 2. Sew together as shown and press. Make 4. **Fig. B**

5. Arrange all units to form a Cat's Cradle block, as shown. Sew the units into rows and press. **Fig. C**

6. Sew together the rows and press. Make 20.

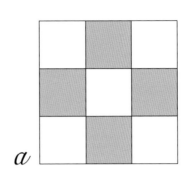

a

b

Make 4.

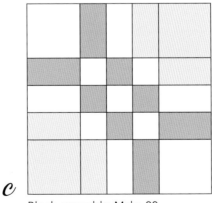

c

Block assembly. Make 20.

PUT IT TOGETHER

1. Arrange the Cat's Cradle blocks into 5 rows of 4 blocks, as shown. Sew the block into rows and press.

2. Sew the rows together and press.

BORDER

1. Measure the length of the quilt in several places to determine the average length. Trim 2 border strips to match your measurement and sew to the right and left sides of the quilt. Press.

2. Repeat this process for the top and bottom borders.

FINISH

Baste, quilt, and bind using your preferred method, or refer to Finishing the Quilt (page 124).

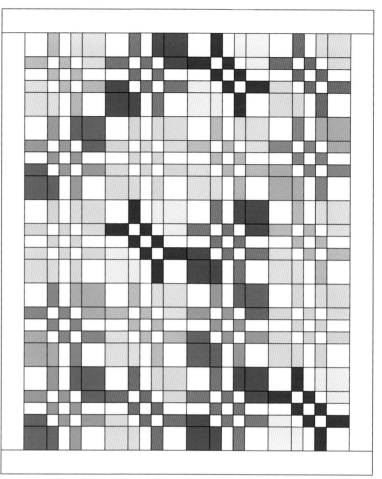

Quilt assembly

SNOWFALL

finished block: 18″ × 18″ • *finished quilt:* 70″ × 70″

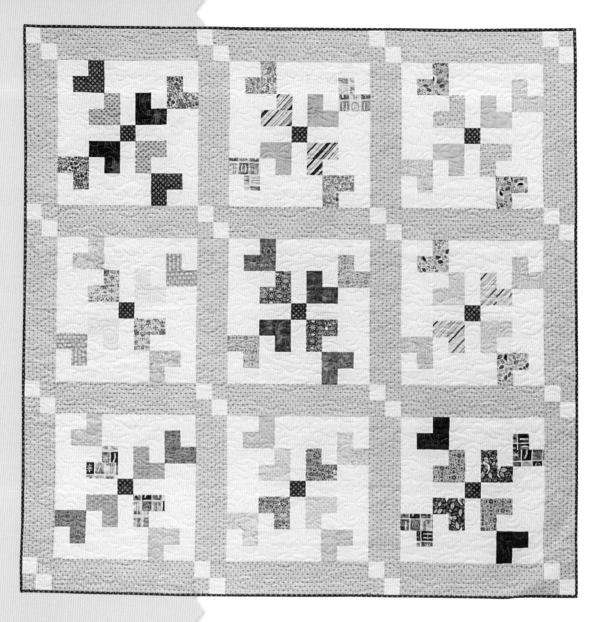

pieced by
Vanessa Goertzen

quilted by
Abby Latimer

*Fabric: Evergreen
by BasicGrey
for Moda Fabrics*

$\mathcal{I}$ think *every child loves snow. There is something magical about going outside to experience the quiet as a blanket of snow muffles the ordinary sounds of the neighborhood. I remember learning in school that each snowflake is different from all the others. Now I live in a place where we rarely have snow. Making a snowflake quilt is a great way to bring the magic into the house. Just as each snowflake is different, the colors of the scrappy little snowflakes in this quilt give variety throughout.*

materials

2 charm packs *or* 6 fat quarters *or* scraps

1 fat eighth of red fabric

2½ yards of white fabric

1⅞ yards of sashing fabric

4½ yards of backing fabric

¾ yard of binding fabric

78″ × 78″ batting

cutting

For the blocks

2 charm packs

- Organize the charm pack squares by print (there will be multiples of 2). Sort into 36 pairs and subcut each pair into 2 rectangles 2½″ × 4½″ and 2 squares 2½″ × 2½″.

6 fat quarters

From each fat quarter:

- Cut 3 strips 2½″ × 22″; subcut each strip into 4 rectangles 2½″ × 4½″.

- Cut 2 strips 2½″ × 22″; subcut each strip into 6 squares 2½″ × 2½″.

Scraps

- Gather or cut 36 sets, with each set containing 2 rectangles 2½″ × 4½″ and 2 squares 2½″ × 2½″ of the same (or a similar) print.

Red fabric

- Cut 2 strips 2½″ × 22″; subcut into 9 squares 2½″ × 2½″.

CUTTING IT UP ✂

This quilt uses 72 squares 5″ × 5″. Whether the 5″ × 5″ squares come from charm packs, fat quarters, or scraps, sort them into 36 matching pairs. Subcut each pair into:

2 rectangles 2½″ × 4½″

2 squares 2½″ × 2½″

White fabric

- Cut 9 strips 4½″ × WOF. Subcut into 4½″ × 8½″ rectangles, 4 per strip, until you have 36.

- Cut 7 strips 2½″ × WOF. Subcut into 2½″ × 2½″ squares, 16 per strip, until you have 104.

- Cut 9 strips 2½″ × WOF. Subcut into 2½″ × 4½″ rectangles, 8 per strip, until you have 72.

Sashing fabric

- Cut 12 strips 4½″ × WOF. Subcut into 4½″ × 18½″ rectangles, 2 per strip, until you have 24.

- Cut 2 strips 2½″ × WOF. Subcut into 2½″ × 2½″ squares, 16 per strip, until you have 32.

Binding fabric

- Cut 8 strips 2½″ × WOF.

construction ‍

Seam allowances are ¼˝ unless otherwise noted. Press the seams toward the darker print. Sew fabrics with right sides together.

MAKE THE BLOCKS

Snowfall Block

1. To make 1 block, gather the following:

1 set of 2 rectangles 2½˝ × 4½˝ and 2 squares 2½˝ × 2½˝ of Print 1

1 set of 2 rectangles 2½˝ × 4½˝ and 2 squares 2½˝ × 2½˝ of Print 2

1 set of 2 rectangles 2½˝ × 4½˝ and 2 squares 2½˝ × 2½˝ of Print 3

1 set of 2 rectangles 2½˝ × 4½˝ and 2 squares 2½˝ × 2½˝ of Print 4

1 red square 2½˝ × 2½˝

8 white squares 2½˝ × 2½˝

8 white rectangles 2½˝ × 4½˝

4 white rectangles 4½˝ × 8½˝

2. Arrange 1 rectangle 2½˝ × 4½˝ of Print 1, 1 square 2½˝ × 2½˝ of Print 1, and 1 white square 2½˝ × 2½˝. Sew the units together as shown and press. Make 2. ***Fig. A***

3. Arrange 1 rectangle 2½˝ × 4½˝ of Print 2, 1 square 2½˝ × 2½˝ of Print 2, and 1 white square 2½˝ × 2½˝. Sew the units together as shown and press. Make 2. ***Fig. B***

4. Retrieve the units from Steps 2 and 3, plus 1 red square 2½˝ × 2½˝ and 4 white rectangles 2½˝ × 4½˝. Arrange all units into a nine-patch as shown. ***Fig. C***

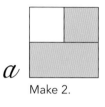

a Make 2.

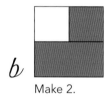

b Make 2.

c

5. Sew the units into rows and press.

6. Sew together the rows and press.

7. Arrange 1 rectangle 2½˝ × 4½˝ of Print 3 and 1 white rectangle 4½˝ × 8½˝ as shown. Sew together and press. Make 2. **Fig. D**

8. Arrange 1 rectangle 2½˝ × 4½˝ of Print 4 and 1 white rectangle 4½˝ × 8½˝ as shown. Sew together and press. Make 2. **Fig. E**

9. Arrange 1 square 2½˝ × 2½˝ of Print 3, 1 white rectangle 2½˝ × 4½˝, and 1 white square 2½˝ × 2½˝, as shown. Sew the units together and press. Make 2. **Fig. F**

10. Arrange 1 square 2½˝ × 2½˝ of Print 4, 1 white rectangle 2½˝ × 4½˝, and 1 white square 2½˝ × 2½˝, as shown. Sew the units together and press. Make 2. **Fig. G**

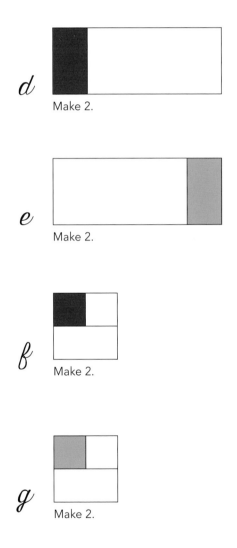

d
Make 2.

e
Make 2.

f
Make 2.

g
Make 2.

11. Arrange the units from Steps 6–10 as shown. Sew the units into their rows and press.

12. Sew together the rows and press. Make 9. *Fig. H*

BORDERS

1. Gather 32 white squares 2½˝ × 2½˝ and 32 sashing fabric squares 2½˝ × 2½˝. Sew these squares together into four-patches as shown and press. Make 16. *Fig. I*

2. Gather 3 rectangles 4½˝ × 18½˝ of sashing fabric and 4 units from Step 1. Arrange the units as shown, sew into a row, and press. Make 4. *Fig. J*

h
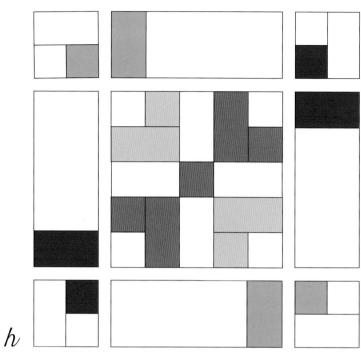
Snowfall block assembly. Make 9.

i
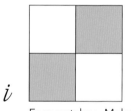
Four-patches. Make 16.

j

Sashing strip. Make 4.

PUT IT TOGETHER

1. Gather the Snowfall blocks, the pieced sashing strips, and the 12 remaining rectangles 4½″ × 18½″ of sashing fabric. Arrange the quilt top as shown. Sew the units into rows and press.

2. Sew the rows together and press.

FINISH

Baste, quilt, and bind using your preferred method, or refer to Finishing the Quilt (page 124).

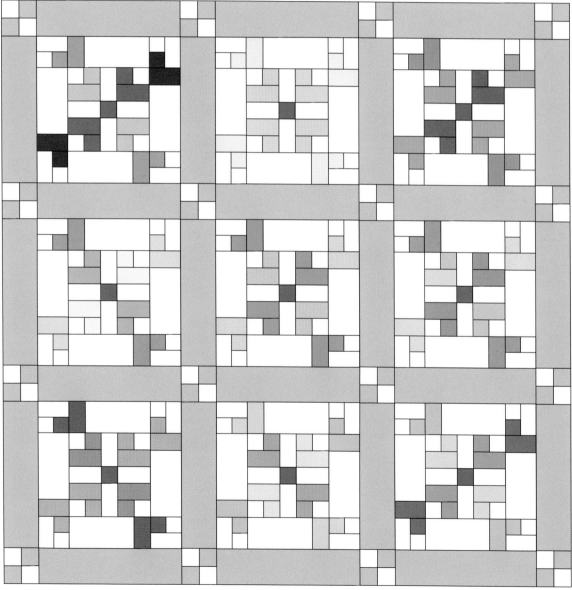

Quilt assembly

easy corner triangles

Let's add triangle shapes. First, try easy corner triangles in the sashing of a simple patchwork quilt in Scrap-Happy (page 49). Then try making Flying Geese blocks—and integrate them into your designs in Up Ahead (page 55) and Solar Eclipse (page 61). Finally, put together all the delightful elements in Madame Butterfly (page 67).

USING CHARM SQUARES

Add easy corner triangles: Mark a diagonal line on a small square and place on the corner of a 5″ × 5″ square, right sides together. Sew along the drawn diagonal line. Trim to a ¼″ seam allowance and press.

 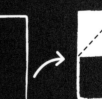

Easy corner triangles open up a new world of options in quilting—Snowball blocks, Flying Geese, and more.

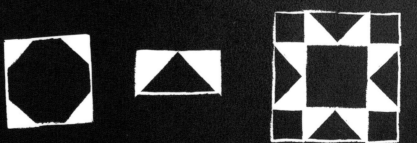

SCRAP-HAPPY

finished block: 16˝ × 16˝ • *finished quilt:* 68½˝ × 68½˝

pieced by
Vanessa Goertzen

quilted by
Abby Latimer

Fabric: Farmhouse
by Fig Tree & Co.
(Joanna Figueroa)
for Moda Fabrics

*H*ere's a quilt designed for the odds and ends in your stash. Maybe you have a collection of mini charm packs you are ready to use, or maybe you have a few pieces of fabric that you just had to buy but didn't really have a quilt in mind for. Find your favorite color to tie it all together. The aqua in this quilt is my favorite—and provides the neutral background. A quilter's stash is more than just a few pieces of fabric. It is inspiration itself! So turn yourself loose and make your own version.

materials

4 charm packs *or* 1 layer cake *or* 1 jelly roll *or* 14 mini charm packs *or* 12 fat quarters *or* scraps

1 yard of cream fabric

2½ yards of sashing fabric

4½ yards of backing fabric

¾ yard of binding fabric

76″ × 76″ batting

cutting

For the blocks

4 charm packs

- Select 144 squares 5″ × 5″; subcut into 576 squares 2½″ × 2½″.

1 layer cake

Select 36 squares 10″ × 10″. From each square:

- Cut 4 strips 2½″ × 10″; subcut each strip into 4 squares 2½″ × 2½″ (to make 16).

1 jelly roll

- Select 36 strips 2½″ × WOF; subcut each strip into 16 squares 2½″ × 2½″.

14 mini charm packs

- No subcutting is needed. You should have 12 leftover squares 2½″ × 2½″.

12 fat quarters

From each fat quarter:

- Cut 6 strips 2½″ × 22″; subcut each strip into 8 squares 2½″ × 2½″ (to make 48).

Scraps

- Cut or gather 576 squares 2½″ × 2½″.

Cream fabric

- Cut 8 strips 2½″ × WOF. Subcut into 2½″ × 2½″ squares, 16 per strip, until you have 128.

- Cut 2 strips 4½″ × WOF. Subcut into 4½″ × 4½″ squares, 8 per strip, until you have 16.

CUTTING IT UP ✂

This quilt uses 576 squares 2½″ × 2½″. The large number of squares suggests the use of a lot of additional options for where we get our fabric from—layer cakes, jelly rolls, and even mini charm packs, in addition to the charm packs, fat quarters, or scraps.

Sashing fabric

- Cut 12 strips 4½″ × WOF. Subcut into 4½″ × 16½″ rectangles, 2 per strip, until you have 24.

- Cut 6 strips 2½″ × WOF. Subcut into 2½″ × 16½″ rectangles, 2 per strip, until you have 12.

- Cut 2 strips 2½″ × WOF. Subcut into 2½″ × 4½″ rectangles, 8 per strip, until you have 16.

- Cut 1 strip 2½″ × WOF. Subcut into 2½″ × 2½″ squares until you have 4.

Binding fabric

- Cut 8 strips 2½″ × WOF.

construction ⌇

Seam allowances are ¼″ unless otherwise noted. Arrows indicate pressing direction. Sew fabrics with right sides together.

MAKE THE BLOCKS

1. To make 1 block, gather 64 assorted print squares 2½″ × 2½″.

2. Arrange 64 squares 2½″ × 2½″ into 8 rows of 8 squares.

3. Sew the squares into rows and press. (Alternate the pressing direction from row to row.)

4. Sew together the rows, nesting the seams together. Press open the seams. Make 9. *Fig. A*

SASHING

1. Retrieve 1 sashing rectangle 4½″ × 16½″ and 2 cream squares 2½″ × 2½″. Mark a diagonal line on the back of each cream square. Place a marked square on 2 opposite corners of the rectangle, with right sides together and the marked line oriented as shown. Sew along the marked line, trim to a ¼″ seam allowance, and press open the seams. *Fig. B*

2. Repeat Step 1 with 2 more squares, placing them in the remaining corners of the rectangle with the marked lines oriented as shown. Sew along the marked lines, trim to a ¼″ seam allowance, and press open the seams. Make 24. *Fig. C*

3. Sew 1 sashing rectangle 2½″ × 16½″ on top of 1 pieced unit from Step 2. Press. Make 12. *Fig. D*

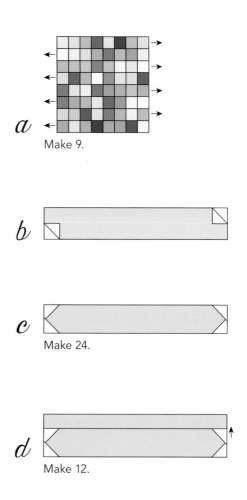

a

Make 9.

b

c

Make 24.

d

Make 12.

Flying Geese

1. Gather 1 sashing rectangle 2½˝ × 4½˝ and 2 cream squares 2½˝ × 2½˝.

2. Mark a diagonal line on the back of each cream square 2½˝ × 2½˝. Align 1 marked cream square along the short edge of 1 sashing rectangle 2½˝ × 4½˝, as shown. Sew along the marked line, trim to a ¼˝ seam allowance, and press open the seam. **Fig. E**

3. Place another cream square on the other side of a unit from Step 2, orienting the marked line as shown. Sew along the marked line, trim to a ¼˝ seam allowance, and press open the seam. Make 16. **Fig. F**

4. Sew together 1 cream square 4½˝ × 4½˝ and 1 unit from Step 3, as shown. Press. Make 12. **Fig. G**

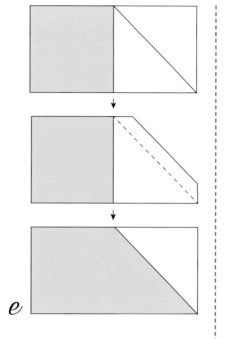

e

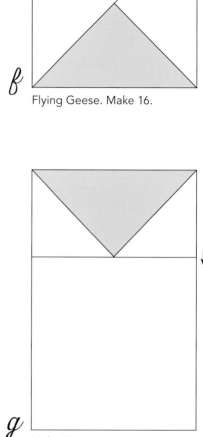

f

Flying Geese. Make 16.

g

Make 12.

PUT IT TOGETHER

1. Arrange all units as shown and sew into rows; press.

2. Sew together the rows and press.

FINISH

Baste, quilt, and bind using your preferred method, or refer to Finishing the Quilt (page 124).

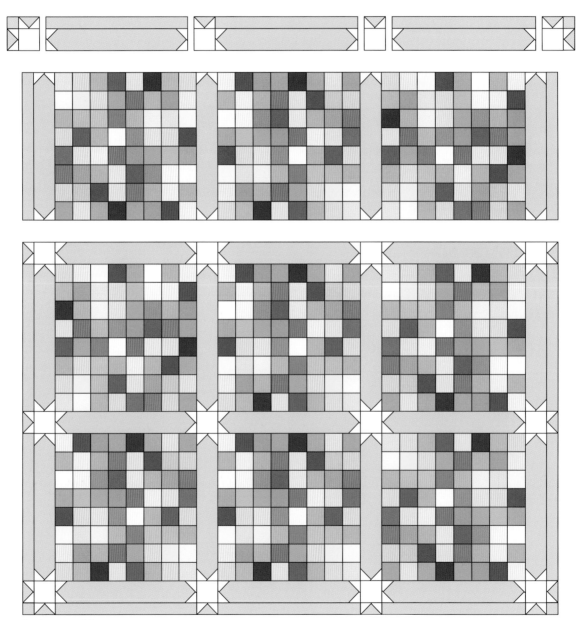

Quilt assembly

UP AHEAD

finished block: 16″ × 16″ • *finished quilt*: 64″ × 80″

pieced by
Vanessa Goertzen

quilted by
Abby Latimer

*Fabric: Fancy & Fabulous
by Fancy Pants Designs
for Riley Blake Designs*

Traveling as a child with my siblings and parents on vacation always involved atlases and maps galore. Now, of course, we have GPS to help us chart a successful path to our destination. While not nearly as charming as signposts and arrows to point us to the next highway, it certainly eliminates guesswork. Up Ahead was inspired by wonderful family trips that included singing along with the Beach Boys, filling up the car (with gas and treats), and laughing from Mad Libs games!

materials

3 charm packs *or* 10 fat quarters *or* scraps

5½ yards of white fabric

5 yards of backing fabric

¾ yard of binding fabric

72″ × 88″ batting

cutting

For the blocks

3 charm packs

- Organize the charm squares by print (there will be multiples of 3). Select 40 sets of 3. For each set, subcut each 5″ × 5″ square into 2 rectangles 2½″ × 4½″ until you have 6 per set.

10 fat quarters

From each fat quarter:

- Cut 6 strips 2½″ × 22″ and subcut each strip into 4 rectangles 2½″ × 4½″ until you have 24. Sort those into 4 sets of 6 per print. Repeat with remaining fat quarters until you have 40 sets total.

Scraps

- Cut or gather 40 sets of 6 rectangles 2½″ × 4½″. Each set should contain 6 of the same (or a similar) print.

White fabric

- Cut 40 strips 2½″ × WOF. Subcut into 2½″ × 2½″ squares, 16 per strip, until you have 640.

- Cut 20 strips 4½″ × WOF. Subcut into 4½″ × 16½″ rectangles, 2 per strip, until you have 40.

Binding fabric

- Cut 8 strips 2½″ × WOF.

CUTTING IT UP

This quilt uses 240 rectangles 2½″ × 4½″. Whether the 2½″ × 4½″ rectangles come from charm squares, fat quarters, or scraps, you will need them organized into 40 sets of 6 rectangles 2½″ × 4½″, with each set containing 6 of the same print.

construction

Seam allowances are ¼˝ unless otherwise noted. Press open seam allowances unless otherwise directed. Sew fabrics with right sides together.

MAKE THE BLOCKS

Flying Geese

1. To make 1 block, gather the following:

6 rectangles 2½˝ × 4½˝ of Print 1

6 rectangles 2½˝ × 4½˝ of Print 2

32 white squares 2½˝ × 2½˝

2 white rectangles 4½˝ × 16½˝

2. Mark a diagonal line on the back of 2 white squares 2½˝ × 2½˝. Align a white square with the short edge of a rectangle 2½˝ × 4½˝ of Print 1, orienting the marked line as shown. Sew along the marked line, trim to a ¼˝ seam allowance, and press open the seam. **Fig. A**

3. Place another white square on the opposite side of the unit from Step 1, orienting the marked line as shown. Sew along the marked line, trim to a ¼˝ seam allowance, and press open the seam. Make 6. **Figs. B & C**

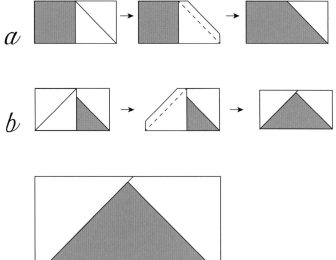

a

b

c

Flying Geese. Make 6.

4. Arrange 6 Flying Geese with 4 white squares 2½˝ × 2½˝, as shown. Sew the units into rows and press open the seams.

5. Sew together the rows and press open the seams. *Fig. D*

6. Repeat Steps 2–5 using 16 marked white squares 2½˝ × 2½˝ and 6 rectangles 2½˝ × 4½˝ of Print 2.

7. Join the units from Steps 5 and 6 vertically and press open the seam. Attach the 2 white rectangles 4½˝ × 16½˝ to the left and right side. Press the seams toward the white fabric. Make 20. *Fig. E*

d

e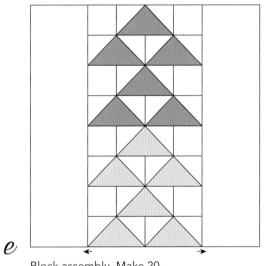

Block assembly. Make 20.

PUT IT TOGETHER

1. Arrange 20 blocks into 5 rows of 4 blocks, alternating the direction of each block as shown.

2. Sew the blocks into rows and press.

3. Sew together the rows and press.

FINISH

Baste, quilt, and bind using your preferred method, or refer to Finishing the Quilt (page 124).

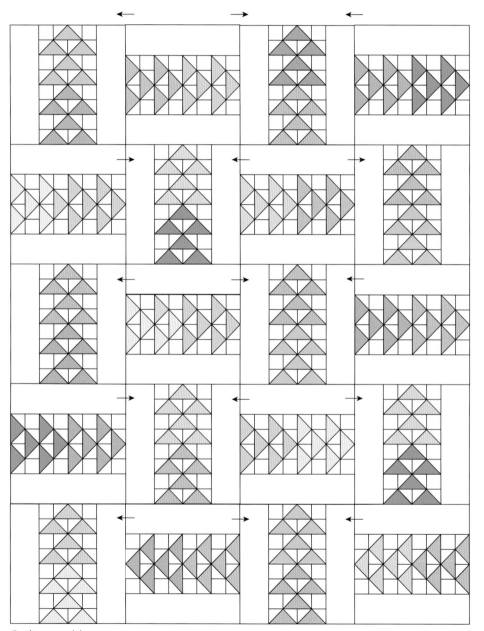

Quilt assembly

Charm School—18 Quilts from 5˝ Squares

SOLAR ECLIPSE

finished block: 8″ × 8″ • *finished quilt:* 60″ × 76″

pieced by
Vanessa Goertzen

quilted by
Abby Latimer

Fabric: Little Miss Sunshine
by Lella Boutique
for Moda Fabrics

𝒯here is something awe inspiring about the sun and earth lining up so perfectly as to produce a solar or lunar eclipse. Here, the ring of light around the shadow of the earth has been translated into quilt form. The colorful rings of light around each shadow offer a perfect contrast between dark and light. Contrast is a very important to the design of this quilt. Vary the temperatures of the colors and the balance of light and dark to make it a stunning addition to your home.

materials

3 charm packs *or* 8 fat quarters *or* scraps

4⅛ yards of navy fabric

¾ yard of pale blue accent fabric

4¾ yards of backing fabric

¾ yard of binding fabric

68″ × 84″ batting

cutting

For the blocks

3 charm packs

- Organize the charm squares by print (there will be multiples of 3). Sort into 32 sets of 3. From each set, subcut 2 squares 5″ × 5″ into 4 rectangles 2½″ × 4½″ and 1 square 5″ × 5″ into 4 squares 2½″ × 2½″.

8 fat quarters

From each fat quarter:

- Cut 4 strips 2½″ × 22″ and subcut each into 4 rectangles 2½″ × 4½″; you will have 16. Cut 2 strips 2½″ × 22″ and subcut each into 8 squares 2½″ × 2½″; you will have 16. Sort into 32 sets, with each set containing 4 rectangles 2½″ × 4½″ and 4 squares 2½″ × 2½″ of the same print.

Scraps

- Cut or gather 32 sets, with each set containing 4 rectangles 2½″ × 4½″ and 4 squares 2½″ × 2½″ of the same (or a similar) print.

CUTTING IT UP ✂

This quilt uses 96 squares 5″ × 5″. Whether the 5″ × 5″ squares come from charm packs, fat quarters, or scraps, you will need them organized into 32 sets of 3 squares 5″ × 5″, with the squares in each set of the same print.

Navy fabric

- Cut 8 strips 8½″ × WOF. Subcut into 8½″ × 8½″ squares, 4 per strip, and 1 rectangle 8½″ × 4½″ until you have 32 squares and 8 rectangles.

- Cut 3 strips 2½″ × WOF. Subcut into 2½″ × 12½″ rectangles, 3 per strip, until you have 8.

- Cut 1 strip 2½″ × WOF. Subcut into 2½″ × 4½″ rectangles until you have 4.

- Cut 24 strips 2½″ × WOF. Subcut into 2½″ × 2½″ squares, 16 per strip, until you have 384.

Pale blue accent fabric

- Cut 4 strips 4½″ × WOF. Subcut into 4½″ × 4½″ squares, 8 per strip, until you have 31.

Binding fabric

- Cut 8 strips 2½″ × WOF.

construction

Seam allowances are ¼″ unless otherwise noted.
Press as directed. Sew fabrics with right sides together.

MAKE THE BLOCKS

1. To make 1 block, gather the following:

1 navy square 8½″ × 8½″

12 navy squares 2½″ × 2½″

4 rectangles 2½″ × 4½″ of Print 1

4 squares 2½″ × 2½″ of Print 1

Snowball Blocks

Mark a diagonal line on the back of 4 squares 2½″ × 2½″ of Print 1. Align a marked print square with a navy square 8½″ × 8½″, orienting the marked line as shown. Sew along the marked line, trim to a ¼″ seam allowance, and press the seam toward the navy square. **Fig. A**

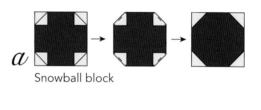

a Snowball block

Flying Geese

1. Mark a diagonal line on the back of 2 navy squares 2½″ × 2½″. Align a marked navy square with a rectangle 2½″ × 4½″ of Print 1. Sew along the marked line, trim to a ¼″ seam allowance, and press the seam toward the navy print. Attach the other marked navy square to the opposite side as shown, sew along the marked line, trim to a ¼″ seam allowance, and press the seam toward the navy print. Make 4. **Fig. B**

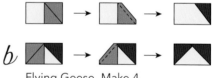
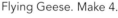

b Flying Geese. Make 4.

2. Gather 1 Snowball block, 2 Flying Geese, and 4 navy squares 2½″ × 2½″. Sew the units into rows, as shown, and press the seams toward the navy squares. **Fig. C**

3. Sew together the rows and press the seams toward the Flying Geese. Make 32. The remaining Flying Geese will be used in Put It Together, Step 3 (next page).

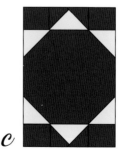

c Block assembly. Make 32.

PUT IT TOGETHER

1. Arrange the units into 7 columns, as shown. (Columns 1, 3, 5, and 7 have 5 units in them. Columns 2, 4, and 6 have 4 units.) *Fig. D*

2. Arrange 31 pale blue accent squares 4½″ × 4½″, as shown. *Fig. E*

3. Place the remaining Flying Geese units adjacent to the pale blue accent squares. Use the matching prints to form the sun shapes. Fill the left and right sides that are still empty with 8 navy rectangles 2½″ × 4½″.

4. Fill the top and bottom sides that are empty with 6 navy rectangles 4½″ × 8½″. *Fig. F*

5. Sew the pieces from Steps 2, 3, and 4 together, and then sew the units into columns.

6. Sew together the columns.

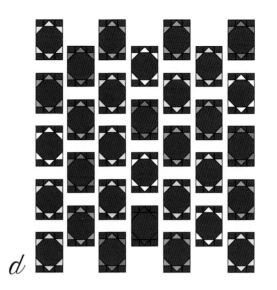

d

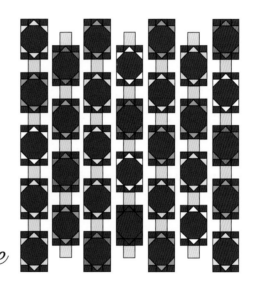

e

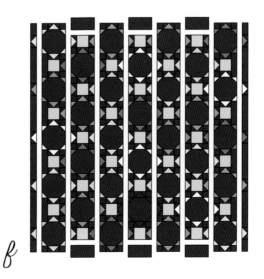

f

7. Add 2 more columns to the outside by using matching Flying Geese units, 4 navy rectangles 2½˝ × 4½˝, and 8 navy rectangles 2½˝ × 12½˝. Sew the units into columns and attach them to the sides of the quilt top.

FINISH

Baste, quilt, and bind using your preferred method, or refer to Finishing the Quilt (page 124).

Quilt assembly

Charm School—18 Quilts from 5˝ Squares

MADAME BUTTERFLY

finished block: 9″ × 9″ • *finished quilt:* 45″ × 57″

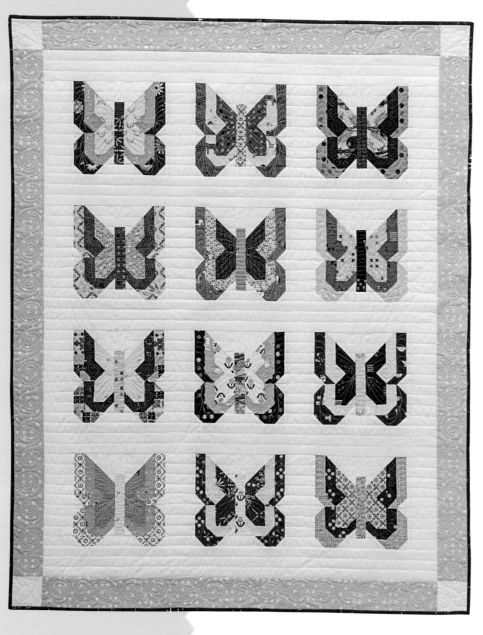

pieced by
Vanessa Goertzen

quilted by
Miriam Rawson

*Fabrics: Honeymoon by
Sarah Watts, Lucky Strikes by
Kimberly Kight, Paper Bandana
by Alexia Marcelle Abegg, Picnic
by Melody Miller, and Zephyr
by Rashida Coleman-Hale for
Cotton + Steel*

*What little girl hasn't caught her breath when
she's seen a beautiful butterfly in a flower garden?
There is something so fairylike about those delicate
wings, which look as though an artist painted them.
Create your own painterly wings by making this wall-
hanging or baby quilt. There are a lot of parts to this
quilt, so organize carefully and follow the directions
to make your own breathtaking piece of art.*

materials

3 charm packs *or* scraps

1¾ yards of white fabric

⅝ yard of border fabric

3¼ yards of backing fabric

½ yard of binding fabric

53″ × 65″ batting

cutting

For the blocks

3 charm packs

- Organize the charm squares by print (there will be multiples of 3). Select 36 sets of 3 squares 5″ × 5″.

Scraps

- Cut or gather 36 sets of 3 squares 5″ × 5″, with each set containing 3 squares of the same (or a similar) print.

SORT AND SUBCUT

- Sort and subcut the 36 sets of 3 into the following groups:

  12 sets of 3 squares 5″ × 5″ for wing exteriors

  12 sets of 3 squares 5″ × 5″ for wing centers

  12 sets of 2 squares 5″ × 5″ for wing interiors

  12 squares 5″ × 5″ for bodies

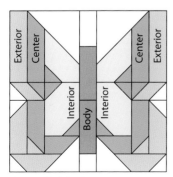

Butterfly block parts

Wing exteriors

- Subcut 1 square 5″ × 5″ into 2 rectangles 1½″ × 4½″ and 2 squares 1½″ × 1½″.

- Subcut 1 square 5″ × 5″ into 3 rectangles 1½″ × 3½″.

- Subcut 1 square 5″ × 5″ into 1 rectangle 1½″ × 3½″ and 2 rectangles 1½″ × 2½″.

Wing centers

- Subcut 1 square 5″ × 5″ into 2 rectangles 1½″ × 4½″ and 2 rectangles 1½″ × 2½″.

- Subcut 1 square 5″ × 5″ into 2 rectangles 1½″ × 3½″.

- Subcut 1 square 5″ × 5″ into 8 squares 1½″ × 1½″.

Wing interiors

- Subcut 1 square 5″ × 5″ into 2 rectangles 2½″ × 4½″.

- Subcut 1 square 5″ × 5″ into 2 rectangles 2½″ × 3½″.

Bodies

- Subcut 1 square 5″ × 5″ into 2 rectangles 1½″ × 3½″.

cutting continued on page 70

CUTTING IT UP ✂

This quilt uses 108 squares 5″ × 5″. Whether the 5″ × 5″ squares come from charm squares or scraps, you will need them sorted into 36 sets of 3 squares 5″ × 5″, with the squares in each set of the same print.

TIP

Keep all pieces organized by print.

White fabric

- Cut 4 strips 3½″ × WOF. Subcut into 3½″ × 9½″ rectangles, 4 per strip, until you have 16.

- Cut 5 strips 3½″ × WOF.

- Cut 3 strips 3½″ × WOF. Subcut into 3½″ × 3½″ squares, 11 per strip, until you have 28.

- Cut 2 strips 2½″ × WOF. Subcut into 2½″ × 2½″ squares, 16 per strip, until you have 24.

- Cut 1 strip 1½″ × WOF. Subcut into 1½″ × 2½″ rectangles until you have 12.

- Cut 4 strips 1½″ × WOF. Subcut into 1½″ × 1½″ squares, 26 per strip, until you have 84.

Border fabric

- Cut 5 strips 3½″ × WOF.

Binding fabric

- Cut 6 strips 2½″ × WOF.

construction

Seam allowances are ¼″ unless otherwise noted. Press open seam allowances unless otherwise directed. Sew fabrics with right sides together.

MAKE THE BLOCKS

1. To make 1 block, gather the following:

Wing Exteriors

From Print 1:

2 rectangles 1½″ × 4½″

4 rectangles 1½″ × 3½″

2 rectangles 1½″ × 2½″

2 squares 1½″ × 1½″

Wing Centers

From Print 2:

2 rectangles 1½″ × 4½″

2 rectangles 1½″ × 3½″

2 rectangles 1½″ × 2½″

8 squares 1½″ × 1½″

Wing Interiors

From Print 3:

2 rectangles 2½″ × 4½″

2 rectangles 2½″ × 3½″

Body

From Print 4:

2 rectangles 1½″ × 3½″

White Fabric

2 squares 3½″ × 3½″

2 squares 2½″ × 2½″

1 rectangle 1½″ × 2½″

7 squares 1½″ × 1½″

2. Gather 2 body rectangles 1½˝ × 3½˝ in Print 4, 1 white square 1½˝ × 1½˝, and 1 white rectangle 1½˝ × 2½˝. Arrange the pieces into 1 row as shown and sew together. Press. *Fig. A*

note ➤——➤

Easy Corner Triangles

In the following steps, you will mark designated squares and place them right sides together according to the diagrams. Pay attention to the orientation of the marked lines, as they are mirrored within each set. Once everything is placed correctly, stitch along the marked lines, trim to a ¼˝ seam allowance, and press.

3. Mark a diagonal line on the back of 2 squares 1½˝ × 1½˝ of Print 2. Sew 1 marked square to each rectangle 2½˝ × 4½˝ of Print 3, as shown. *Fig. B*

4. Sew 1 rectangle 1½˝ × 4½˝ of Print 2 to the outside of each unit from Step 3. Press. *Fig. C*

5. Sew 1 rectangle 1½˝ × 4½˝ of Print 1 to the outside of each unit from Step 4. Press. *Fig. D*

6. Mark a diagonal line on the back of 2 white squares 3½˝ × 3½˝. Sew 1 marked white square to each unit from Step 5 as shown. Press. *Fig. E*

7. Mark a diagonal line on the back of 4 squares 1½˝ × 1½˝ of Print 2. Sew 2 marked squares to 1 rectangle 2½˝ × 3½˝ of Print 3, as shown. Press. *Fig. F*

8. Sew 1 rectangle 1½˝ × 2½˝ of Print 2 to bottom of each unit from Step 7, as shown. Press. *Fig. G*

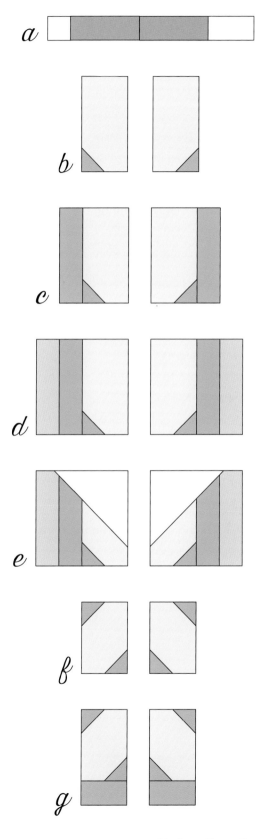

9. Mark a diagonal line on the back of 2 white squares 1½″ × 1½″. Sew 1 marked white square to each 1½″ × 2½″ rectangle of Print 1. Press. **Fig. H**

10. Mark a diagonal line on the back of 2 squares 1½″ × 1½″ of Print 2. Sew 1 marked square to each unit from Step 9, as shown. Press. **Fig. I**

11. Mark a diagonal line on the back of 2 squares 1½″ × 1½″ of Print 1. Sew to each 1½″ × 3½″ rectangle of Print 2. Press. **Fig. J**

12. Sew 1 rectangle 1½″ × 3½″ of Print 1 to each unit from Step 11, as shown. Press. **Fig. K**

13. Mark a diagonal line on the back of 2 white squares 1½″ × 1½″. Sew 1 marked white square to each unit from Step 12, as shown. Press. **Fig. L**

14. Sew 1 unit from Step 10 to the top of each unit from Step 13, as shown. Press. **Fig. M**

15. Sew 1 unit from Step 14 to each unit from Step 8, as shown. Press. **Fig. N**

16. Mark a diagonal line on the back of 2 white squares 1½″ × 1½″. Sew 1 marked white square to each remaining rectangle 1½″ × 3½″ of Print 1. Press. **Fig. O**

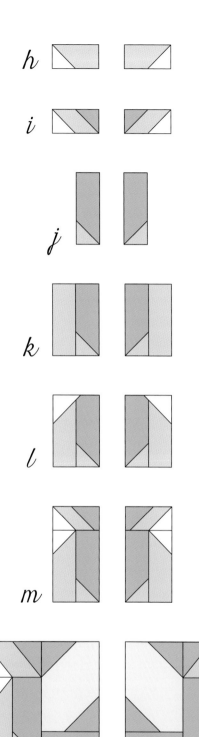

17. Sew each unit from Step 16 to each unit from Step 15, as shown. Press. *Fig. P*

18. Sew each unit from Step 17 to each unit from Step 6, as shown. Press. *Fig. Q*

19. Mark a diagonal line on the back of 2 white squares 2½″ × 2½″. Sew 1 marked white square to each unit from Step 18, as shown. Press. *Fig. R*

20. Sew the units from Step 19 and Step 2 together, as shown. Make 12 blocks. *Fig. S*

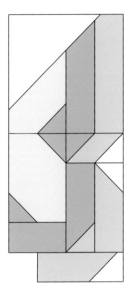

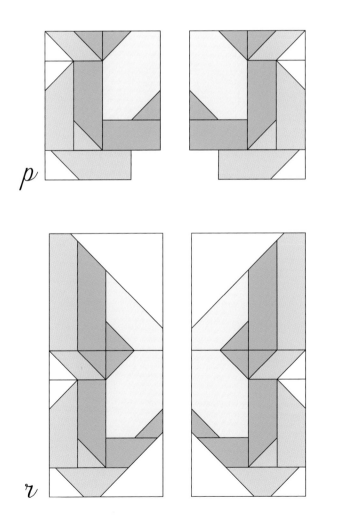

p

q

r

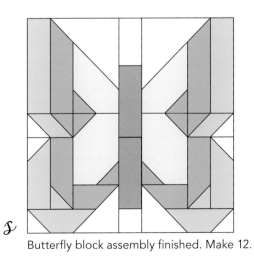

s

Butterfly block assembly finished. Make 12.

PUT IT TOGETHER

1. Arrange the Butterfly blocks into 4 rows of 3 blocks. Sew the blocks into rows with 1 white rectangle 3½″ × 9½″ in between and on the outside, as shown. Press. *Fig T*

2. Verify that each row measures 39½″ wide. Once confirmed, trim 5 white strips 3½″ × WOF to 3½″ × 39½″ (or to fit the width of your row). Sew the rows together with 1 white strip in between and on the top and bottom.

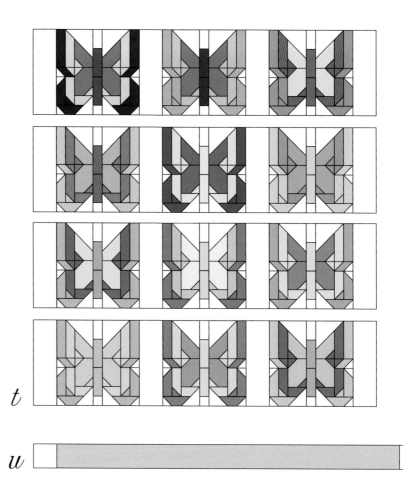

t

u

BORDER

1. Measure the width of your quilt in several places and determine the average. Trim 2 border strips to this length and sew to the top and bottom of the quilt. Press.

2. Determine the length of the quilt by measuring in several places, disregarding the border. Cut 2 border pieces to this length and sew a white 3½″ × 3½″ square to each end of the border strips. Sew to each side. Press. *Fig. U*

FINISH

Baste, quilt, and bind using your preferred method, or refer to Finishing the Quilt (page 124).

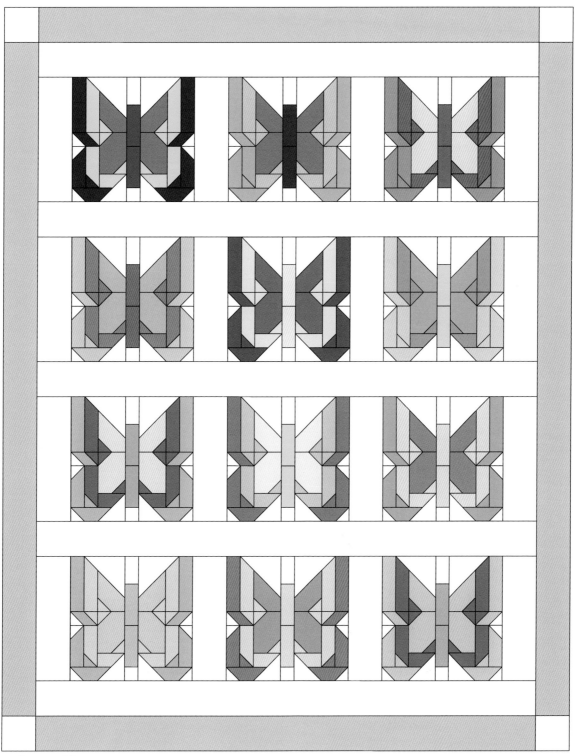

Quilt assembly

half-square triangles

In the previous section, you added triangle shapes to existing blocks with an easy corner triangle method. Now let's make individual triangle units called Half-Square Triangles. We'll employ two different techniques using our 5″ × 5″ squares to get two different sizes of Half-Square Triangles.

Transform 5″ × 5″ squares into large Half-Square Triangle blocks, and incorporate them in Rock Star (page 77), First Crush (page 82), and Hoodwink (page 92) using the first method. Or make smaller Half-Square Triangle blocks (but twice as many) with the second method, and use them to make Charm Bracelet (page 87).

No matter which method you prefer, you will find that adding Half-Square Triangles to your quilting repertoire brings exciting new shapes into view.

USING CHARM SQUARES

Mark a diagonal line on the back of a 5″ × 5″ square and bring it right sides together with another 5″ × 5″ square. Sew ¼″ away from both sides of the marked line. Cut along the marked line, press, and trim to 4½″ × 4½″. Makes 2 Half-Square Triangle blocks.

Mark an X on the back of a light 5″ × 5″ square. Place it right sides together with another 5″ × 5″ square. Sew all the way around the perimeter, ¼″ away from the outside edges. Cut on the marked lines, press, and trim each unit to 3″ × 3″. Makes 4 Half-Square Triangle blocks.

ROCK STAR

finished block: 12″ × 12″ • *finished quilt:* 69″ × 81″

pieced and quilted by
Vanessa Goertzen

*Fabric: Fresh Cut
by BasicGrey
for Moda Fabrics*

*D*o you remember your first rock concert? Think of the spectacle—the bright lights, the outrageous volume, and the thrill of seeing your idol live on stage. This quilt is sure to make your heart skip a beat with its funky color scheme and untraditional layout. Half-Square Triangles are the real star of this design. Grab your Bloc Loc ruler and get this show on the road.

materials

3 charm packs *or* 10 fat quarters *or* scraps

3 yards of cream fabric

1¼ yards of border fabric

5 yards of backing fabric

¾ yard of binding fabric

77″ × 89″ batting

cutting

For the blocks

3 charm packs

- Organize the charm squares by print (there will be multiples of 3). Select 38 matching pairs and set them aside. Select 38 squares 5″ × 5″ (for the star centers) and trim each to 4½″ × 4½″.

10 fat quarters

From each fat quarter:

- Cut 2 strips 5″ × 22″ and subcut into 8 squares 5″ × 5″. Organize the 5″ × 5″ squares into 38 matching pairs. There will be extra. Cut 1 strip 4½″ × 22″ and subcut each into 4 squares 4½″ × 4½″ until you have 38.

Scraps

- Cut or gather 38 matching pairs of 5″ × 5″ squares and 38 squares 4½″ × 4½″.

Cream fabric

- Cut 10 strips 5″ × WOF. Subcut into 5″ × 5″ squares, 8 per strip, until you have 76.

- Cut 4 strips 4½″ × WOF. Subcut into 1 rectangle 4½″ × 20½″ per strip, until you have 4. From the excess, cut 4 rectangles 4½″ × 8½″.

- Cut 7 strips 4½″ × WOF. Subcut into 4½″ × 4½″ squares, 8 per strip, until you have 52.

CUTTING IT UP

This quilt uses 114 squares 5″ × 5″. Whether the 5″ × 5″ squares come from charm packs, fat quarters, or scraps, sort them into 38 sets of 2, with each set containing 2 of the same print. Set aside another 38 squares 5″ × 5″ for the star centers.

Border fabric

- Cut 8 strips 5″ × WOF. Piece together in pairs along the short sides to make 4 border strips.

Binding fabric

- Cut 9 strips 2½″ × WOF.

construction

Seam allowances are ¼″ unless otherwise noted. Press open seam allowances unless otherwise directed. Sew fabrics with right sides together.

MAKE THE BLOCKS

Friendship Star Blocks

1. To make 1 block, gather the following:

    2 squares 5″ × 5″ of Print 1

    2 cream squares 5″ × 5″

2. Mark a diagonal line on the back of 1 cream square 5″ × 5″ and place right sides together with 1 square 5″ × 5″ of Print 1. Sew ¼″ away from the marked line on both sides. Cut along the marked line, press toward the dark side, and trim each Half-Square Triangle block to 4½″ × 4½″. Make 4 per print until you have 38 sets of 4 Half-Square Triangles. *Fig. A*

3. Gather 4 Half-Square Triangles of Print 1 and 1 square 4½″ × 4½″ of Print 2. Arrange into Friendship Stars, as shown. Sew the units of the middle row together and press. Make 38. *Fig. B*

-------------------- TIP --------------------

Perfect Trimming

For perfectly trimmed 4½″ × 4½″ Half-Square Triangle blocks, use the 4½″ Bloc Loc ruler. Just press each Half-Square Triangle seam to the darker fabric, lock the ruler in place on top, and trim.

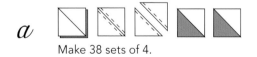

a

Make 38 sets of 4.

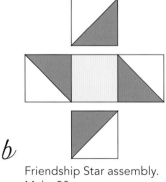

b

Friendship Star assembly.
Make 38.

PUT IT TOGETHER

1. Arrange the Friendship Star sets into columns, beginning on the left side and moving to the right, staggering the columns as shown. *Fig. C*

2. Add the cream squares and rectangles where there are spaces.

3. Sew the units into rows and press.

4. Sew together the rows and press.

BORDER

1. Measure the length of the quilt in several places to determine the average. Trim 2 pieced border strips to match your measurement and sew to the right and left sides of the quilt. Press.

2. Repeat this process for the top and bottom borders.

FINISH

Baste, quilt, and bind using your preferred method, or refer to Finishing the Quilt (page 124).

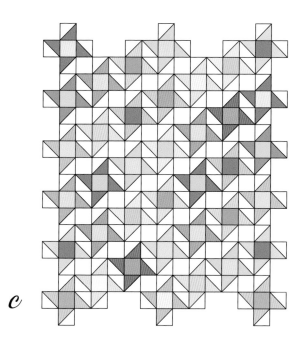

Quilt assembly

FIRST CRUSH

finished block: 12″ × 12″ • *finished quilt*: 72″ × 84″

materials

3 charm packs *or* 11 fat quarters *or* scraps

2½ yards of white fabric

2 yards of blue fabric

5¼ yards of backing fabric

¾ yard of binding fabric

80″ × 92″ batting

cutting

For the blocks

3 charm packs

- Organize the charm squares by print (there will be multiples of 3) until you have 42 sets of 3.

11 fat quarters

From each fat quarter:

- Cut 3 strips 5″ × 22″ and subcut into 4 squares 5″ × 5″ per strip (to total 12). Organize into 42 sets of 3 by print. There will be extra.

Scraps

- Cut or gather 42 sets of 5″ × 5″ squares, with each set containing 3 squares of the same (or a similar) print.

White fabric

- Cut 16 strips 5″ × WOF. Subcut into 5″ × 5″ squares, 8 per strip, until you have 126.

Blue fabric

- Cut 11 strips 4½″ × WOF. Subcut into 4½″ × 8½″ rectangles, 4 per strip, and 4½″ × 4½″ squares until you have 42 rectangles and 15 squares.

- Cut 4 strips 4½″ × WOF. Subcut into 4½″ × 4½″ squares, 8 per strip, until you have 27.

Binding fabric

- Cut 9 strips 2½″ × WOF.

CUTTING IT UP

This quilt uses 126 squares 5″ × 5″. Whether the 5″ × 5″ squares come from charm packs, fat quarters, or scraps, sort them into 42 sets of 3, with each set containing 3 of the same print.

pieced by
Vanessa Goertzen

quilted by
Abby Latimer

Fabric: Gooseberry
by Lella Boutique
for Moda Fabrics

𝓕irst crushes are usually a mix of sweet memories and a few jagged edges. I remember when I had a crush on Robbie in junior high. I confided this to some friends, and one of them immediately yelled, "Robbie, Vanessa has a big crush on you!" Of course he never spoke to me again. Unlike my first crush, I promise this quilt story will have a happy ending.

construction

Seam allowances are ¼″ unless otherwise noted. Press open seam allowances unless otherwise directed. Sew fabrics with right sides together.

MAKE THE BLOCKS

Half-Square Triangles

1. To make 1 block, gather the following:

   3 squares 5″ × 5″ of Print 1

   3 white squares 5″ × 5″

   1 blue square 4½″ × 4½″

   1 blue rectangle 4½″ × 8½″

2. Mark a diagonal line on the back of the 3 white squares 5″ × 5″ and place right sides together with each 5″ × 5″ square of Print 1. Sew ¼″ away from the marked line on both sides. Cut along the marked line, press toward the darker fabric, and trim each Half-Square Triangle unit to 4½″ × 4½″. Make 6. **Fig. A**

a

Make 6.

------------------------------ TIP ------------------------------

Tool Tip

*The 4½″ Bloc Loc ruler makes quick work
of squaring up Half-Square Triangle blocks.*

----

3. Arrange the 6 units with 1 blue square 4½″ × 4½″ and 1 blue rectangle 4½″ × 8½″ into rows, as shown.

4. Sew the units into rows and press.

5. Sew together the rows and press. Make 42. **Fig. B**

b

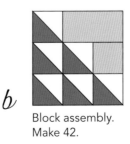

Block assembly.
Make 42.

PUT IT TOGETHER

1. Arrange 42 blocks into 7 rows of 6 blocks, as shown.

2. Sew the blocks into rows and press.

3. Sew the rows together and press.

FINISH

Baste, quilt, and bind using your preferred method, or refer to Finishing the Quilt (page 124).

Quilt assembly

CHARM BRACELET

finished block: 13½˝ × 13½˝ • *finished quilt:* 64˝ × 79½˝

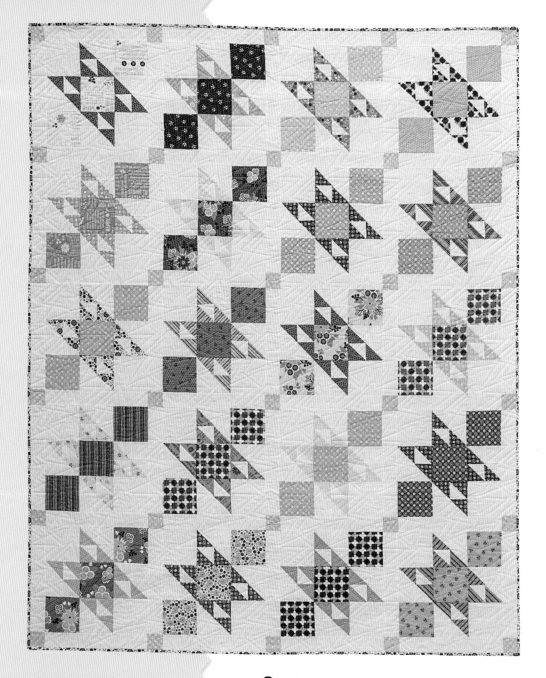

pieced by
Vanessa Goertzen

quilted by
Abby Latimer

Fabric: Meadowbloom
by April Rosenthal of
Prairie Grass Patterns
for Moda Fabrics

My daughter, Olive, recently discovered the world of jewelry, and she has her own collection—including a favorite charm bracelet. She also strings together colorful beads and baubles to create necklaces and bracelets for her friends and family. Swapping fabric squares for beads, you can create a charming treasure for those you love.

materials

3 charm packs *or* 10 fat quarters *or* scraps

3¾ yards of white fabric

¼ yard of taupe fabric

5 yards of backing fabric

¾ yard of binding fabric

72″ × 88″ batting

cutting

For the blocks

3 charm packs

- Organize the charm squares by print (there will be multiples of 3) until you have 40 sets of 3.

10 fat quarters

From each fat quarter:

- Cut 3 strips 5″ × 22″ and subcut into 4 squares 5″ × 5″ per strip (to total 12). Organize into 40 sets of 3 by print.

Scraps

- Cut or gather 40 sets of 3 squares 5″ × 5″ squares, with each set containing 3 squares of the same (or a similar) print.

White fabric

- Cut 13 strips 5″ × WOF. Subcut into 5″ × 5″ squares, 8 per strip, until you have 100. Cut 1 rectangle 2½″ × 14″ from the remaining strip.

- Cut 6 strips 2¾″ × WOF. Subcut into 2¾″ × 2¾″ squares, 14 per strip, until you have 80.

- Cut 3 strips 14″ × WOF. Subcut into 2½″ × 14″ rectangles, 16 per strip, until you have 48.

CUTTING IT UP

This quilt uses 120 squares 5″ × 5″. Whether the 5″ × 5″ squares come from charm packs, fat quarters, or scraps, sort them into 40 sets of 3, with each set containing 3 of the same print.

Taupe fabric

- Cut 2 strips 2½″ × WOF. Subcut into 2½″ × 2½″ squares, 16 per strip, until you have 30.

Binding fabric

- Cut 8 strips 2½″ × WOF.

construction ❧

Seam allowances are ¼˝ unless otherwise noted. Press open seam allowances unless otherwise directed. Sew fabrics with right sides together.

MAKE THE BLOCKS

To make 1 block, gather the following:

    3 squares 5˝ × 5˝ of Print 1

    3 squares 5˝ × 5˝ of Print 2

    5 white squares 5˝ × 5˝

    4 white squares 2¾˝ × 2¾˝

Half-Square Triangles

1. Mark an X on the back of 3 white squares 5˝ × 5˝. Place one of them right sides together with a 5˝ × 5˝ square of Print 2. Sew the squares together by stitching ¼˝ away from the raw edges around the perimeter. Cut along the marked X, press toward the dark print, and trim each small Half-Square Triangle to 2¾˝ × 2¾˝. Make 12. **Fig. A**

2. Arrange 3 of the Half-Square Triangles with 1 white square 2¾˝ × 2¾˝, as shown.

3. Sew the units into rows and press.

4. Sew together the rows and press. Make 4. **Fig. B**

5. Arrange the units with 2 white squares 5˝ × 5˝ and 3 squares 5˝ × 5˝ of Print 1, as shown.

6. Sew the units into rows and press.

7. Sew together the rows and press. Make 20. **Fig. C**

a

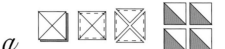

Half-Square Triangles. Make 12.

b

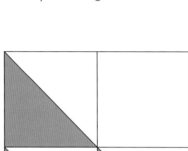

Make 4.

c

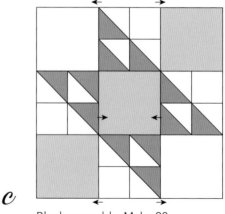

Block assembly. Make 20.

PUT IT TOGETHER

1. Sew together 4 white rectangles 2½″ × 14″ and 5 taupe squares 2½″ × 2½″, as shown. Press toward the white fabric. Make 6.

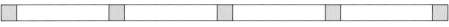

Pieced sashing row. Make 6.

2. Arrange 20 blocks into 5 rows of 4 blocks, as shown.

3. Sew the blocks into rows with 1 white rectangle 2½″ × 14″ in between and on the sides. Press toward the white fabric.

4. Sew together the quilt block rows and the pieced sashing rows, as shown. Press toward the sashing rows.

FINISH

Baste, quilt, and bind using your preferred method, or refer to Finishing the Quilt (page 124).

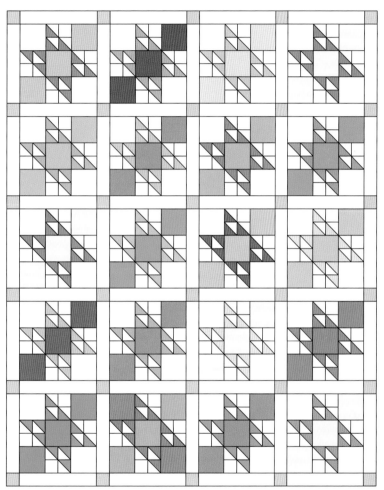

Quilt assembly

HOODWINK

finished block: 16″ × 16″ • *finished quilt:* 69″ × 69″

materials

3 charm packs *or* 9 fat quarters *or* scraps

2⅛ yards of white fabric

1½ yards of cream sashing fabric

1¼ yards of border fabric

4½ yards of backing fabric

¾ yard of binding fabric

77″ × 77″ batting

cutting

For the blocks

3 charm packs

- Organize the charm squares by print (there will be multiples of 3) until you have 36 sets of 3. From each set, subcut 1 square into 4 squares 2½″ × 2½″.

9 fat quarters

From each fat quarter:

- Cut 3 strips 5″ × 22″ and subcut into 4 squares 5″ × 5″ per strip (to total 12). Organize into 36 sets of 3 by print. From each set, subcut 1 square into 4 squares 2½″ × 2½″.

Scraps

- Cut or gather 36 sets, with each set containing 2 squares 5″ × 5″ and 4 squares 2½″ × 2½″ of the same (or a similar) print.

White fabric

- Cut 9 strips 5″ × WOF. Subcut into 5″ × 5″ squares, 8 per strip, until you have 72.

- Cut 9 strips 2½″ × WOF. Subcut into 2½″ × 2½″ squares, 16 per strip, until you have 144.

CUTTING IT UP

This quilt uses 108 squares 5″ × 5″. Whether the 5″ × 5″ squares come from charm packs, fat quarters, or scraps, sort them into 36 sets of 3, with each set containing 3 of the same print.

Cream sashing fabric

- Cut 6 strips 3½″ × WOF. Subcut into 3½″ × 16½″ rectangles, 2 per strip, until you have 12.

- Cut 8 strips 3½″ × WOF. Piece the strips together in pairs.

Border fabric

- Cut 8 strips 5″ × WOF. Piece the strips together in pairs along their short sides to make 4 border strips.

Binding fabric

- Cut 8 strips 2½″ × WOF.

pieced by
Vanessa Goertzen

quilted by
Abby Latimer

Fabric: Mon Ami
by BasicGrey
for Moda Fabrics

When my parents were away, my oldest brother would babysit us and show us magic tricks. Sometimes he would tell us the secret behind an illusion, and it would suddenly seem obvious. We all felt quite foolish, of course, for not discovering the secret on our own. Sometimes quilting can be the same way—once you come to understand the framework of a quilt, it becomes easy! These sporty little quilt blocks are really quite fun to make once you understand the simple techniques behind them.

construction

Seam allowances are ¼″ unless otherwise noted. Press open the seam allowances unless otherwise directed. Sew fabrics with right sides together.

MAKE THE BLOCKS

To make 1 block, gather the following:

  2 squares 5″ × 5″ of Print 1

  4 squares 2½″ × 2½″ of Print 1

  2 white squares 5″ × 5″

  4 white squares 2½″ × 2½″

Half-Square Triangles

1. Mark a diagonal line on the back of 1 white square 5″ × 5″. Place right sides together with 1 square 5″ × 5″ of Print 1. Sew ¼″ away from the marked line on both sides. Cut along the marked line, and press toward the dark print. Square-up each Half-Square Triangle to 4½″ × 4½″. Make 4. *Fig. A*

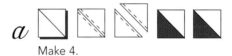

a Make 4.

------------------ **TIP** ------------------

Handy Help

The 4½″ Bloc Loc ruler makes it easy to trim perfect Half-Square Triangle blocks.

----

2. Mark a diagonal line on the back of 4 white squares 2½″ × 2½″. Place one of them atop a Half-Square Triangle, aligning the marked square in the corner of Print 1, as shown. Sew along the marked line, trim to a ¼″ seam, and press. Make 4. *Fig. B*

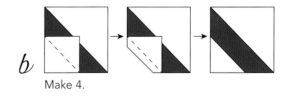

b Make 4.

3. Mark a diagonal line on the back of 4 squares 2½″ × 2½″ of Print 1. Place one of them atop a unit from Step 2, aligning the marked square in the white corner opposite the triangle added in Step 2. Sew along the marked line, trim to a ¼″ seam, and press. Make 4. **Fig. C**

4. Arrange 4 units into a diamond formation, as shown. Sew the units into rows and press.

5. Sew together the rows and press. Make 36. **Fig. D**

6. Select 4 units and arrange into 2 rows of 2 units. Sew the units into rows and press.

7. Sew together the rows and press. Make 9. **Fig. E**

PUT IT TOGETHER

1. Arrange 9 blocks into 3 rows of 3 blocks, as shown.

2. Add sashing between the blocks and on the sides, using 4 cream rectangles 3½″ × 16½″ for each row. Press toward the cream sashing.

3. Trim each pieced sashing strip to the length of the row (it should be 3½″ × 60½″). Sew together the quilt block rows and the pieced sashing rows, as shown. Press toward the sashing.

c

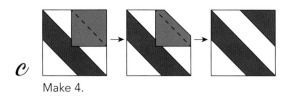

Make 4.

d

Make 36.

e

Block assembly. Make 9.

BORDER

1. Measure the length of the quilt in several places to determine the average. Trim 2 border strips to match your measurement and sew to the right and left sides of the quilt. Press.

2. Repeat the process for the top and bottom borders.

FINISH

Baste, quilt, and bind using your preferred method, or refer to Finishing the Quilt (page 124).

Quilt assembly

quarter-square triangles

Now that you've made Half-Square Triangle blocks, you can go one step further and make them into Quarter-Square Triangle blocks, as in Somersault (page 99) and Love Letter (page 104).

The Quarter-Square Triangle is another important building block that adds variety to a design. They always remind me of dapper little bow ties, and I love finding ways to insert them into my quilts.

USING CHARM SQUARES

Mark a diagonal line on the back of a 5″ × 5″ square and bring it right sides together with another 5″ × 5″ square. Sew ¼″ away from both sides of the marked line. Cut along the marked line, press, and trim to 4½″ × 4½″. Makes 2 Half-Square Triangle blocks.

Mark a diagonal line on the back of a 4½″ × 4½″ Half-Square Triangle. Place it right sides together with another 4½″ × 4½″ Half-Square Triangle—darker print right sides together with the lighter print. Sew ¼″ away from both sides of the marked line. Cut along the marked line, press, and trim to 4″ × 4″. Makes 2 Quarter-Square Triangle blocks.

SOMERSAULT

finished block: 10½˝ × 10½˝ • *finished quilt:* 63˝ × 74½˝

pieced by
Vanessa Goertzen

quilted by
Abby Latimer

*Fabric: Daysail
by Bonnie & Camille
for Moda Fabrics*

Who can refrain from smiling when seeing a little child try to do a somersault? When they first learn, they remind me of a primitive wheel, more angular than round. As they grow older, they start to be more daring—rolling down grassy hills—like a scene in The Princess Bride. *This quilt captures the primitive motion of an early somersault and comes together in a jiffy.*

materials

3 charm packs *or* 9 fat quarters *or* scraps

3 yards of white fabric

1½ yards of navy fabric

4¾ yards of backing fabric

¾ yard of binding fabric

71″ × 83″ batting

cutting

For the blocks

3 charm packs

- Organize the charm squares by print (there will be multiples of 3). Select 42 matching pairs and subcut each square to 4″ × 4″. From the remaining 5″ × 5″ charm squares, select 21 and set them aside.

9 fat quarters

From each fat quarter:

- Cut 2 strips 4″ × 22″ and subcut each into 5 squares 4″ × 4″ (to total 10). Cut 1 strip 5″ × 22″. Subcut into 3 squares 5″ × 5″ and set them aside. There will be extra.

Scraps

- Cut or gather 42 pairs of 4″ × 4″ squares of the same (or a similar) print. Cut or gather 21 assorted squares 5″ × 5″ and set them aside.

White fabric

- Cut 11 strips 4½″ × WOF. Subcut into 4½″ × 4½″ squares, 8 per strip, until you have 84.

- Cut 9 strips 4″ × WOF. Subcut into 4″ × 4″ squares, 10 per strip, until you have 84.

- Cut 3 strips 5″ × WOF. Subcut into 5″ × 5″ squares, 8 per strip, until you have 21.

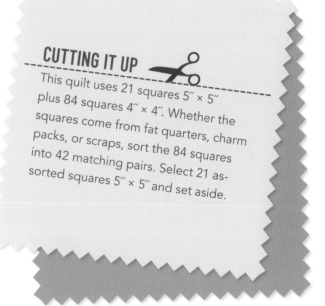

CUTTING IT UP

This quilt uses 21 squares 5″ × 5″ plus 84 squares 4″ × 4″. Whether the squares come from fat quarters, charm packs, or scraps, sort the 84 squares into 42 matching pairs. Select 21 assorted squares 5″ × 5″ and set aside.

Navy fabric

- Cut 11 strips 4½″ × WOF. Subcut into 4½″ × 4½″ squares, 8 per strip, until you have 84.

Binding fabric

- Cut 8 strips 2½″ × WOF.

construction ♪

Seam allowances are ¼″ unless otherwise noted. Press toward the darker print unless noted otherwise. Sew fabrics with right sides together.

MAKE THE BLOCKS

Navy Half-Square Triangles

Gather 84 white squares 4½″ × 4½″ and 84 navy squares 4½″ × 4½″. Mark a diagonal line on the back of the white squares. Place one of them atop a navy square. Sew ¼″ away from the marked line on both sides. Cut along the marked line, press the seam toward the navy, and trim each Half-Square Triangle to 4″ × 4″. Make 168. **Fig. A**

Print Half-Square Triangles

Gather 21 assorted print squares 5″ × 5″ and 21 white squares 5″ × 5″. Mark a diagonal line on the back of each white square. Place one of them atop a print square. Sew ¼″ away from the marked line on both sides. Cut along the marked line, press the seam toward the print, and trim each Half-Square Triangle to 4½″ × 4½″. Make 42. **Fig. B**

Print Quarter-Square Triangles

Mark a diagonal line on the back of 1 Half-Square Triangle and align it with 1 unmarked Half-Square Triangle of the same print so that the print halves face the white halves. Sew ¼″ away from the marked line on both sides. Cut along the marked line, press open the seam, and trim each Quarter-Square Triangle to 4″ × 4″. Make 42. **Fig. C**

Nine-Patches

Gather the following to make 1 block:

  2 squares 4″ × 4″ of Print 1

  2 white squares 4″ × 4″

  4 navy Half-Square Triangles 4″ × 4″

  1 Quarter-Square Triangle 4″ × 4″ of Print 2

1. Arrange all the units into a Nine-Patch, as shown.

2. Sew the units into rows and press open.

3. Sew together the rows and press open. Make 42. **Fig. D**

a

Navy Half-Square Triangle. Make 168.

b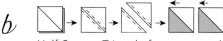

Half-Square Triangle from assorted prints. Make 42.

c

Quarter-Square Triangle. Make 42.

d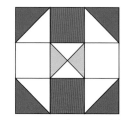

Nine-Patch assembly. Make 42.

PUT IT TOGETHER

1. Sew the blocks into 7 rows of 6 blocks, alternating the orientation of the blocks as shown. Alternate the pressing direction of each row.

2. Sew together the rows and press.

FINISH

Baste, quilt, and bind using your preferred method, or refer to Finishing the Quilt (page 124).

Quilt assembly

LOVE LETTER

finished block: 10½˝ × 10½˝ • *finished quilt:* 52˝ × 66½˝

materials

3 charm packs *or* 10 fat quarters *or* scraps

1¼ yards of white fabric

1¾ yards of cream sashing and border fabric

3½ yards of backing fabric

⅝ yard of binding fabric

60″ × 75″ batting

cutting

For the blocks

3 charm packs

- Organize the charm squares by print. (There will be multiples of 3.) Select 20 sets of 3 and subcut according to the Group A instructions. Subcut the other 20 sets of 3 according to the Group B instructions.

5 fat quarters (Group A)

From each fat quarter:

- Cut 4 strips 2¼″ × 22″. Subcut into 2¼″ × 4″ rectangles, 4 per strip, until you have 16.

- Cut 2 strips 2¼″ × 22″. Subcut into 2¼″ × 2¼″ squares, 8 per strip, until you have 16.

5 fat quarters (Group B)

From each fat quarter:

- Cut 2 strips 5″ × 22″. Subcut into 5″ × 5″ squares, 4 per strip, until you have 8.

- Cut 1 strip 4″ × 22″. Subcut into 4″ × 4″ squares until you have 4.

Scraps

- Cut or gather 120 squares 5″ × 5″ so there are multiples of 3 per print. Sort into 40 sets of 3. Subcut 20 sets of 3 according to the Group A instructions. Subcut 20 sets of 3 according to the Group B instructions.

White fabric

- Cut 5 strips 5″ × WOF. Subcut into 5″ × 5″ squares, 8 per strip, until you have 40.

- Cut 5 strips 2¼″ × WOF. Subcut into 2¼″ × 2¼″ squares, 17 per strip, until you have 80.

cutting continued
on page 107

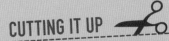

CUTTING IT UP

This quilt uses 120 squares 5″ × 5″. Whether the squares come from charm packs, fat quarters, or scraps, sort them into 40 sets of 3, with each set containing 3 of the same print. Divide the sets into 2 groups of 20 sets to make Groups A and B, which will be subcut as follows:

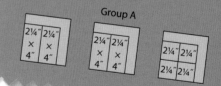

Group A: For each matching set of 3 squares 5″ × 5″, subcut into 4 rectangles 2¼″ × 4″ and 4 squares 2¼″ × 2¼″.

Group A

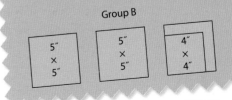

Group B: For each matching set of 3 squares, keep 2 squares 5″ × 5″ and trim the remaining square to 4″ × 4″.

Group B

pieced by
Vanessa Goertzen

quilted by
Abby Latimer

*Fabric: Miss Scarlet
by Minick & Simpson
for Moda Fabrics*

Even if it isn't Valentine's Day, red and white are delightful. Think of a small cottage with white, cream, and pink wallpaper; lace at the windows; and this beautiful quilt draped over a wrought-iron bed. Now picture yourself in that comfy space, reading your favorite book, next to a red tray holding a pot of fresh peppermint tea ready to sip. Think of this quilt as a love letter to yourself.

Cream sashing and border fabric

- Cut 2 strips 4½″ × WOF. Subcut into 4½″ × 11″ rectangles, 3 per strip, until you have 4.

- Cut 7 strips 2½″ × WOF. Subcut into 2½″ × 11″ rectangles, 3 per strip, until you have 20.

- Cut 10 strips 2½″ × WOF. Piece the strips together in pairs along their short sides to make 5 border strips.

Binding fabric

- Cut 7 strips 2½″ × WOF.

---

construction

Seam allowances are ¼″ unless otherwise noted. Press seam allowances toward the darker fabric. Sew fabrics with right sides together.

MAKE THE BLOCKS

Gather the following to make 1 block:

2 white squares 5″ × 5″

1 set of Group A (4 rectangles 2¼″ × 4″ and 4 squares 2¼″ × 2¼″ of Print 1)

1 set of Group B (2 squares 5″ × 5″ and 1 square 4″ × 4″ of Print 2)

4 white squares 2¼″ × 2¼″

Half-Square Triangles

Mark a diagonal line on the back of 1 white square 5″ × 5″. Place right sides together with 1 square 5″ × 5″ from Group B. Sew 1/4″ away from the marked line on both sides. Cut along the marked line, press, and trim each Half-Square Triangle to 4½″ × 4½″. Make 4. **Fig. A**

Quarter-Square Triangles

1. Mark a diagonal line on the back of 1 Half-Square Triangle and align it with 1 unmarked Half-Square Triangle of the same print so that the print halves face the white halves. Sew ¼″ away from the marked line on both sides. Cut along the marked line, press open the seams, and trim each Quarter-Square Triangle to 4″ × 4″. Make 4. **Fig. B**

2. Sew 1 white square 2¼″ × 2¼″ to 1 square 2¼″ × 2¼″ from Group A. Make 4. **Fig. C**

a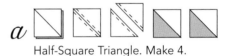
Half-Square Triangle. Make 4.

b
Quarter-Square Triangle. Make 4.

c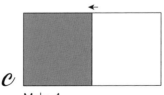
Make 4.

3. Add 1 rectangle 2¼″ × 4″ from Group A to 1 unit from Step 2. Make 4. *Fig. D*

4. Gather 4 Quarter-Square Triangles, 4 units from Step 3, and 1 square 4″ × 4″ from Group B. Arrange as shown and sew the units into rows. Press. *Fig. E*

5. Sew the rows together and press. Make 20. *Fig. F*

PUT IT TOGETHER

1. Arrange the blocks in 4 columns of 5 blocks, as shown. Sew the blocks into columns with 1 cream rectangle 2½″ × 11″ in between to connect them. Sew 1 cream rectangle to the top of columns 1 and 3 and to the bottom of columns 2 and 4. Press the seams.

2. Sew 1 cream rectangle 4½″ × 11″ to the bottom of columns 1 and 3 and to the top of columns 2 and 4. Press the seams.

3. Measure the length of each column (which should measure 67″) and take the average. Trim each of the pieced cream strips to match the average length of your columns. Sew together the columns with cream strips in between each column and on each outer side. Press the seams.

FINISH

Baste, quilt, and bind using your preferred method, or refer to Finishing the Quilt (page 124).

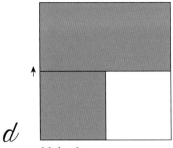

d Make 4.

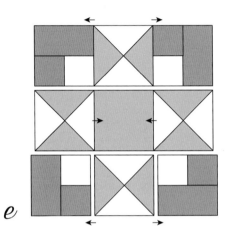

e

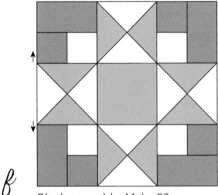

f Block assembly. Make 20.

Quilt assembly

wonky talk

Congratulations! You've learned the basics of using 5″ × 5″ squares. Now add an element of whimsy to your quilts by employing wonky cuts and tricks. These projects begin with simply pieced, traditional blocks, but you'll see how adding tilts and angles makes them look unpredictable.

USING CHARM SQUARES

Make your favorite traditional blocks using 5″ × 5″ squares. Add an unexpected twist by framing the blocks with triangles cut from rectangles, as in *Tipsy* (page 111).

Stack a traditional block on top of a solid square of the same size and make wonky cuts. Swap the pieces and stitch them back together, as in *Lunch Box* (page 117).

TIPSY

finished block: 11″ × 11″ • *finished quilt:* 66″ × 77″

pieced by
Vanessa Goertzen

quilted by
Abby Latimer

*Fabrics: Aunt Grace Basics,
Aunt Grace Simpler Sampler,
and Gracie's Schoolhouse
Classics
by Judie Rothermel
for Marcus Fabrics*

J think most little girls dream of becoming ballerinas. I recall going to a production of The Nutcracker with my first-grade class. When I got home, I twirled around the house, rose up onto my tiptoes, and believed I was just as graceful as the dancers on stage. I was woefully ignorant of my lack of technique and experience—until I went to a dance teacher and began to learn proper techniques. With this project you will add wedge-shaped pieces to scrappy sawtooth stars and teach them to dance!

---

materials

3 charm packs *or* 11 fat quarters or scraps

2½ yards of white fabric

3 yards of yellow fabric

5 yards of backing fabric

¾ yard of binding fabric

74″ × 85″ batting

---

cutting

For the blocks

3 charm packs

- Organize the charm squares by print (there will be multiples of 3). Sort them into 42 matching pairs. From each pair, subcut 2 squares 5″ × 5″ into 8 squares 2½″ × 2½″. Trim the remaining 42 squares 5″ × 5″ to 4½″ × 4½″.

11 fat quarters

From each fat quarter:

- Cut 1 strip 4½″ × 22″ and subcut into 4 squares 4½″ × 4½″.

- Cut 4 strips 2½″ × 22″. Subcut 2½″ × 2½″ squares, 8 per strip, until you have 32.

Scraps

- Cut or gather 42 sets, with each set containing 8 squares 2½″ × 2½″ of the same (or a similar) print. Cut or gather 42 assorted 4½″ × 4½″ squares.

White fabric

- Cut 21 strips 2½″ × WOF. Subcut into 2½″ × 4½″ rectangles, 8 per strip, until you have 168.

- Cut 11 strips 2½″ × WOF. Subcut into 2½″ × 2½″ squares, 16 per strip, until you have 168.

CUTTING IT UP ✂

This quilt uses 126 squares 5″ × 5″. Whether the squares come from charm packs, fat quarters, or scraps, sort them into 42 sets of 2, with each set containing 2 of the same print. For each set, subcut 2 squares 5″ × 5″ into 8 squares 2½″ × 2½″. Trim the remaining 42 assorted squares to 4½″ × 4½″.

Binding fabric

- Cut 8 strips 2½″ × WOF.

cutting continued on page 114

Tipsy **113**

cutting continued on page 114

Yellow fabric

- Cut 7 strips 14″ × WOF. Subcut into 3″ × 14″ rectangles, 13 per strip, until you have 84. Subcut into A Triangles and B Triangles, as shown.

A Triangles

- From 42 rectangles 3″ × 14″, subcut each rectangle into 2 triangles by cutting at a diagonal from the top left corner to the bottom right corner, yielding 84 A Triangles.

Yield 84 A Triangles.

B Triangles

- From 42 rectangles 3″ × 14″, subcut each rectangle into 2 triangles by cutting at a diagonal from the bottom left corner to the top right corner, yielding 84 B Triangles.

Yield 84 B Triangles.

---

construction

Seam allowances are ¼″ unless otherwise noted. Press toward the darker print unless noted otherwise. Sew fabrics with right sides together.

MAKE THE BLOCKS

Sawtooth Star

Gather the following to make 1 block:

1 square 4½″ × 4½″ of Print 1

8 squares 2½″ × 2½″ of Print 2

4 white rectangles 2½″ × 4½″

4 white squares 2½″ × 2½″

FLYING GEESE

1. Mark a diagonal line on the back of 2 squares 2½″ × 2½″ of Print 2. Align 1 marked square with 1 white rectangle 2½″ × 4½″, as shown. Sew along the marked line, trim the seam to ¼″, and press open the seam. **Fig. A**

2. Align 1 marked square with 1 unit from Step 1, as shown. Sew along the marked line, trim the seam to ¼″, and press open the seam. Make 4. **Fig. B**

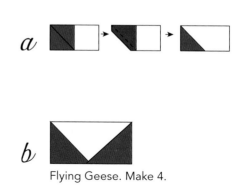

a

b

Flying Geese. Make 4.

3. Arrange the Flying Geese with 4 white squares 2½˝ × 2½˝ and 1 square 4½˝ × 4½˝ of Print 1 into rows, as shown. Sew the units into rows and press toward the white squares. *Fig. C*

4. Sew the rows together and press toward the center row. Make 42. *Fig. D*

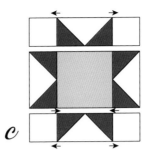

c

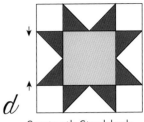

d   Sawtooth Star block assembly. Make 42.

A BLOCKS

1. To make 1 A Block, you will need 1 Sawtooth Star block and 4 A Triangles.

2. Place 1 A Triangle right sides together along the top of 1 Sawtooth Star block, aligning the raw edges on the left side. Partially sew together, leaving the last 2˝ unstitched. Press. *Fig. E*

3. Rotate the block clockwise and add the next triangle in the same manner, except sew all the way across. Press. Repeat for the remaining 2 sides. Finish sewing the partial seam in place. Trim the tails and square up the block to 11½˝ × 11½˝. Make 21. *Fig. F*

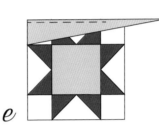

e

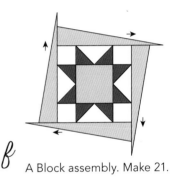

f   A Block assembly. Make 21.

B BLOCKS

1. To make 1 B Block, you will need 1 Sawtooth Star block and 4 B Triangles.

2. Place 1 B Triangle right sides together along the bottom edge of 1 Sawtooth Star block, aligning the raw edges on the bottom left side. Partially sew together, leaving the last 2˝ unstitched. Press. *Fig. G*

3. Rotate the block counterclockwise and add the next triangle in the same manner, except sew all the way across. Press. Repeat for the last 2 sides. Finish sewing the partial seam in place. Trim the tails and square up the block to 11½˝ × 11½˝. Make 21. *Fig. H*

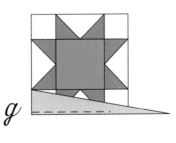

g

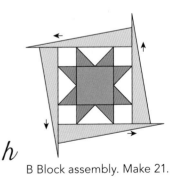

h   B Block assembly. Make 21.

PUT IT TOGETHER

1. Arrange the blocks into 7 rows of 6 blocks, alternating A Blocks and B Blocks, as shown. Sew the blocks into rows and press.

2. Sew together the rows. Press.

FINISH

Baste, quilt, and bind using your preferred method, or refer to Finishing the Quilt (page 124).

Quilt assembly

LUNCH BOX

finished block: 16″ × 16″ • *finished quilt:* 64″ × 80″

pieced by
Vanessa Goertzen

quilted by
Abby Latimer

*Fabric: Serenity
by Amy Ellis
for Moda Fabrics*

This quilt reminds me of days back in elementary school when my friends and I used to cut up our sandwiches and trade them with each other. We all thought it was great fun to have a variety of tastes for lunch, and I even remember a friend recommending that we all try adding potato chips to hers for some extra crunch. When you make this quilt, you will slice up Nine-Patch blocks and swap around the pieces to create a scrappy delight. Grab some charm packs, fat quarters, or your favorite leftovers and get started!

materials

4 charm packs *or* 14 fat quarters *or* scraps

2¾ yards of gray fabric

5 yards of backing fabric

¾ yard of binding fabric

72″ × 88″ batting

cutting

For the blocks

4 charm packs

- Organize the charm squares by print (there will be multiples of 4). Sort into 40 sets of 4. For each set, subcut the following:

  Keep 1 square 5″ × 5″.

  Subcut 1 square 5″ × 5″ into 4 squares 2½″ × 2½″.

  Subcut 2 squares 5″ × 5″ into 4 rectangles 2½″ × 5″.

14 fat quarters

From each fat quarter:

- Cut 3 strips 5″ × 22″. Subcut each strip as shown to get 3 squares 5″ × 5″, 12 rectangles 2½″ × 5″, and 12 squares 2½″ × 2½″.

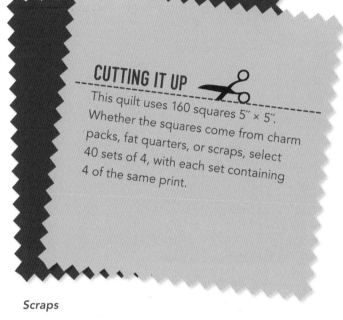

CUTTING IT UP

This quilt uses 160 squares 5″ × 5″. Whether the squares come from charm packs, fat quarters, or scraps, select 40 sets of 4, with each set containing 4 of the same print.

5″	2½″ × 5″	2½″ × 5″	2½″ × 5″	2½″ × 5″	2½″	2½″
					2½″	2½″
5″	2½″ × 5″	2½″ × 5″	2½″ × 5″	2½″ × 5″	2½″	2½″
					2½″	2½″
5″	2½″ × 5″	2½″ × 5″	2½″ × 5″	2½″ × 5″	2½″	2½″
					2½″	2½″

Fat quarter cutting

Scraps

- Cut or gather the following from scraps:

  40 squares 5″ × 5″

  160 squares 2½″ × 2½″ (multiples of 4 per print)

  160 rectangles 2½″ × 5″ (multiples of 4 per print)

Gray fabric

- Cut 10 strips 9″ × WOF. Subcut into 9″ × 9″ squares, 4 per strip, until you have 40.

Binding fabric

- Cut 8 strips 2½″ × WOF.

construction

Seam allowances are ¼″ unless otherwise noted. Press open seam allowances unless otherwise directed. Sew fabrics with right sides together.

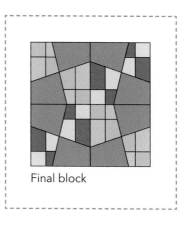

Final block

MAKE THE BLOCKS

Nine-Patch Blocks

1. Gather the following to make 1 block:

1 square 5″ × 5″ of Print 1

4 squares 2½″ × 2½″ of Print 1

4 rectangles 2½″ × 5″ of Print 2

TIP

Spice It Up

Although I have only used two prints in each of my Nine-Patches, feel free to use more variety, experiment with placement, and make yours as scrappy as you like.

---

2. Arrange 1 square 5″ × 5″ of Print 1, 4 squares 2½″ × 2½″ of Print 1, and 4 rectangles 2½″ × 5″ of Print 2 into rows, as shown. Sew the units into rows. Press. *Fig. A*

3. Sew together the rows and press. Verify that each block measures 9″ × 9″, or trim as needed. Make 40. *Fig. B*

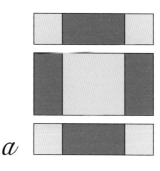

a

b

Nine-Patch block. Make 40.

BLOCK A

1. Using 20 Nine-Patch blocks, make the first wonky cut by lining up 1 block on the grid lines of the cutting mat. Use a ruler to make a diagonal cut 3˝ right of the bottom left corner to 3˝ left of the top right corner. Make a second wonky cut by cutting 3˝ down from the top left corner to 3˝ up from the bottom right corner. *Fig. C*

2. Select 20 gray squares 9˝ × 9˝ and make the same wonky cuts to each by lining up each square on the cutting mat and cutting 3˝ right of the bottom left corner to 3˝ left from the top right corner, and then another cut 3˝ down from the top left corner to 3˝ up from the bottom right corner. *Fig. D*

3. Mix and match the units to form a square, as shown. Sew the units into rows and press toward the gray fabric. *Fig. E*

4. Sew together the rows and press open the seam. Square up if necessary (it should be 8½˝ × 8½˝ unfinished). Make 2. *Fig. F*

c

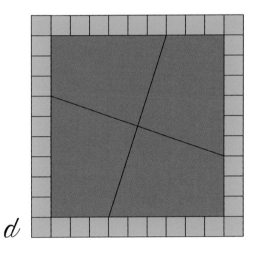

d

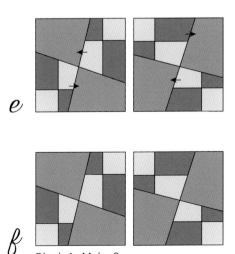

e

f

Block A. Make 2.

BLOCK B

1. For the 20 remaining Nine-Patch blocks, make wonky cuts to mirror those of Block A by lining up 1 block on the grid lines of the cutting mat. Use a ruler to make a diagonal cut 3″ right of the top left corner down to 3″ left of the bottom right corner. Make a second wonky cut by cutting 3″ up from the bottom left corner up to 3″ down from the top right corner. **Fig. G**

2. For the 20 remaining gray squares 9″ × 9″, make the same wonky cuts to each by cutting 3″ right of the top left corner down to 3″ left of the bottom right corner, and then 3″ up from the bottom left corner to 3″ down from the top right corner. **Fig. H**

3. Mix and match the units to form squares. Sew the units into rows and press away from the gray fabric.

4. Sew together the rows and press open the seams. Square up if necessary (it should be 8½″ × 8½″ unfinished). Make 2. **Fig. I**

LUNCH BOX BLOCKS

1. Arrange 2 units of Block A and 2 units of Block B as shown. Sew the units into rows and press open the seams.

2. Sew together the rows and press open the seam. Make 20. **Fig. J**

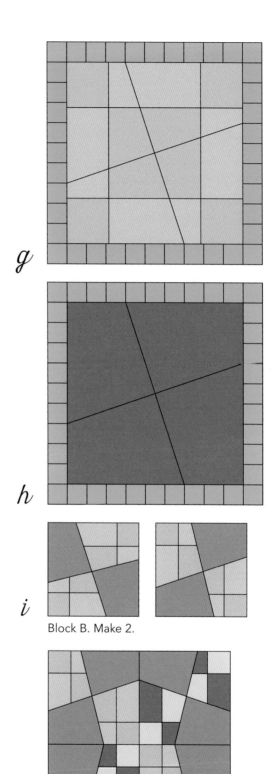

g

h

i

Block B. Make 2.

j

Block assembly. Make 20.

PUT IT TOGETHER

1. Arrange the blocks into 5 rows of 4. Sew the blocks into rows and press.

2. Sew together the rows. Press.

FINISH

Baste, quilt, and bind using your preferred method, or refer to Finishing the Quilt (page 124).

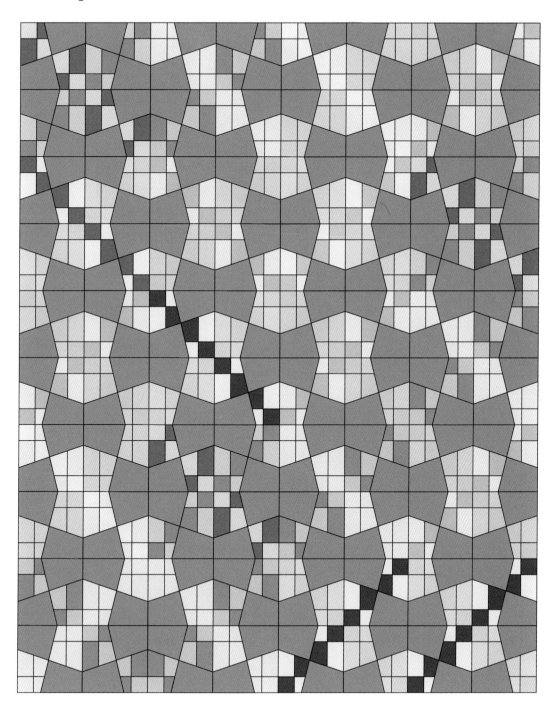

FINISHING THE QUILT

After you have successfully pieced your quilt top, it is ready to be basted, quilted, and bound.

preparing the backing fabric

Plan on making the backing at least 8″ longer and 8″ wider than the quilt top. Piece if necessary.

batting

Choosing batting is a very individual decision. Each type has pros and cons, including how much loft it offers and how closely it needs to be quilted. I love Fairfield Nature-Fil bamboo-blend batting—it is soft and warm, and I love the way it washes and drapes. No matter what you use, cut the batting 8″ longer and 8″ wider than the quilt top. Your batting choice will affect how much quilting is necessary. Be sure to check the manufacturer's recommendations on the packaging to see how far apart the quilting lines can be.

basting

Basting is the process of securing together the quilt top, batting, and backing so that the layers don't shift during the quilting process. (If you plan to send out your quilt for finishing, a longarm quilter will take care of this step.) For domestic machine quilting or hand quilting, work in a clean area large enough to lay out the backing fabric wrong side up. Tape down the edges with masking tape (or use T-pins to secure the backing over a carpeted area). Center the batting on top of the backing, smoothing out any creases. Place the quilt top right side up on top of the batting and backing, making sure it is centered.

For domestic machine quilting, insert safety pins 3″–4″ apart to ensure that the layers won't shift during quilting. For hand quilting, baste together the layers with thread, using a long needle and light-colored thread. Knot one end of the thread. Using stitches approximately the length of the needle, begin in the center and move out toward the edges in vertical and horizontal rows approximately 3″–4″ apart to ensure that the layers won't shift during quilting.

quilting

The quilting process is a way to embellish the quilt with decorative stitching over its entirety—not only adding texture and beauty to your project but also permanently meshing all the layers.

LONGARM QUILTING

It's easy to hire a professional longarm quilter to do this for you. Ask your local quilt shop or guild for recommendations. The cost per quilt varies, depending on the complexity of a project. An allover design usually costs less than a custom design; discuss your options with your quilter. I love the professional quality this adds to my quilts.

DOMESTIC QUILTING

Do it yourself! There is definitely a learning curve to quilting your own projects if you haven't done it before, but with some practice it can be fun and very satisfying. There are many books about free-motion quilting on your home machine—I love Natalia Bonner's book, *Beginner's Guide to Free-Motion Quilting* (by C&T Publishing).

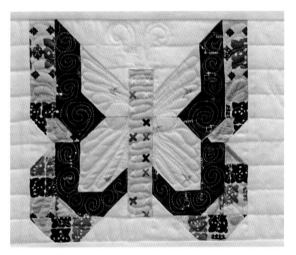

Up Ahead (page 55), quilted by Abby Latimer

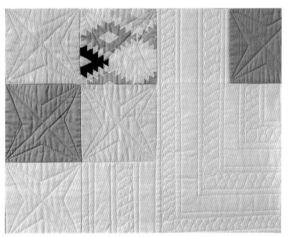

Modern Basic (page 15), quilted by Natalia Bonner

Madame Butterfly (page 67), quilted by Miriam Rawson

binding

My preferred technique for binding a quilt uses a double-fold method. I start out with binding strips cut 2½˝ × the width of fabric. Refer to the specific quilt pattern instructions to see how many strips you will need.

1. Prepare your binding by sewing the 2½˝ strips end to end on the bias to make 1 long strip. Trim the seams to ¼˝ and press open. **Fig. A**

2. Fold the binding in half lengthwise, wrong sides together, and press to keep the fold in place. Starting in the middle of one side of the quilt, line up the raw edges of the binding with the raw edge of the quilt. Skipping the first 8˝ of the binding, use a scant ⅜˝ seam allowance to stitch the binding to the quilt. Stop a scant ⅜˝ away from the end of that side, backstitch, and remove the quilt from the machine. **Fig. B**

3. Fold the binding upward to make a 90° angle, then fold it down to run along the next side of the quilt, raw edges still aligned. Resume stitching from the top of the new side, using the same scant ⅜˝ seam allowance, and stop ⅜˝ from the end of that side. Repeat the fold at all corners. **Fig. C & D**

4. Once you have pivoted at all corners, keep sewing until you are several inches away from the beginning of the binding. Trim the tails to overlap by exactly 2½˝. Unfold the binding tails and bring the right sides together on the bias, as shown. Mark a diagonal line as indicated. Sew along the marked line, trim the ¼˝ seam, and press open the seam. **Fig. E**

5. Fold the binding back in half and pin in place onto the quilt top (it should be an exact fit). Finish stitching the binding in place, using a scant ⅜˝ seam allowance.

6. Bring the folded edge of the binding up and over to the back of the quilt. Pin in place and miter the corners. Stitch the binding in place, using a double-threaded needle.

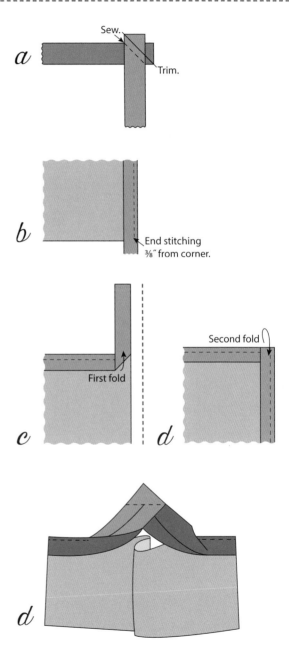

a Sew. Trim.

b End stitching ⅜˝ from corner.

c First fold

d Second fold

d

ABOUT THE AUTHOR

Before Vanessa Goertzen was even born, she was going to quilt shops with her mother. As children, she and her brothers were surrounded by shelves full of quilting fabric, the constant whir of her mother's BERNINA, and piles of patterns ready for mailing. Is it any wonder that she made her first quilt as a teenager?

Vanessa never made any plans to follow in her mother's footsteps, but somehow the fates decided differently. When Vanessa was expecting her first child, she started quilting again. She found that creating her baby girl's first quilt was an intoxicating experience—and she couldn't stop.

In 2010 Vanessa started a pattern company called Lella Boutique, and she has published dozens of quilt and sewing patterns. Vanessa has always been drawn to the beautiful fabrics of Moda, and she began the joyful experience of designing fabric for Moda in 2013 with her debut collection, Into the Woods. Vanessa has two active children, Olive and Lorenzo, who also like making things and always keep life interesting down in southern Utah.

Photo by Peekaboophotos

Want even more creative content?

Make it, snap it, share it *using* #ctpublishing